CW00536311

OASES

OASES
poems and prose

Alastair Reid

CANONGATE

First published in Great Britain
in 1997 by Canongate Books Ltd,
14 High Street, Edinburgh EH1 1TE

British Library Cataloguing-in-Publication Data
A catalogue record for this book is available on
request from the British Library

The publisher acknowledges subsidy from the
Scottish Arts Council towards the publication
of this volume.

ISBN 0 86241 717 1

Typeset by Palimpsest Book Production Limited,
Polmont, Stirlingshire
Printed and bound by
Bookcraft, Midsomer Norton, Somerset

'A man sets himself the task of drawing the world.

As the years pass, he fills the blank page with images of provinces and kingdoms, mountains, bays, ships, islands, fish, houses, instruments, stars, horses, and people. Just before he dies, he discovers that the patient labyrinth of lines traces the image of his own face.'

Jorge Luis Borges

Contents

Oases

Since writing has been my livelihood, and since I have worn a number of different writing hats, as poet, as prose writer, as translator, and as occasional critic, I have left behind me over the years more pieces of writing than I can remember. This collection gathers together some that I think deserve a continuing life.

What drew me always to writing was its portability: it requires essentially no more than a notebook and a pencil, and it allowed me to own my own time, to travel light, to come to rest anywhere, a freedom I made full use of, for I have lived in a number of different countries and languages, and have written about them, inevitably. I travelled mainly to find places to come to rest in, places to write in, oases.

I first left Scotland during the war, the latter part of which I spent at sea, in the East, and after the war, I decided to translate myself to the New World. In New York, I began to publish poems in *The New Yorker*, and later joined the staff of that magazine. It encouraged its writers then to follow their own curiosity, to find their own wave-length; and over the years I published there poems, stories, essays, comment, reviews, translations, and chronicles from different parts of the world. *The*

New Yorker remains my only address, one fixed point in my shifting existence.

New York has been a city I have come to and gone from many times, a city as comfortable to me as old clothes, where I have a web of friends, and a place to write. But the intensity of cities asks for an antidote, and in search of such I went often to live in fairly remote outposts, places with a habitable silence. I had my beginnings in Galloway, a soft green setting that still feels like an oasis to me, and I tended to come to rest in places where I could find the same agrarian rhythm — a water mill in the French Basque country, a sturdy cottage on the far edge of a Spanish mountain village, a small house I built above a faraway beach in the Dominican Republic, where I lived a succession of winters without telephone or shoes. But there were other oases that imprinted themselves deeply — a solitary house by the sea at St Andrews, a patio in Chile, a houseboat on the Thames in London, an *atico* in Barcelona, a corner studio in Greenwich Village, a rooftop perch in Cartagena de Indias, and, occasionally, a house or an inn stayed in for no more than a night or two that I can still inhabit in my memory.

While I live in the spoken language — in conversation, in the web of human connection, in old friendships and new encounters — it is to the written language I turn to clear my head, to find an equilibrium, to discover what I think by seeing what I say. Writing is a strange and solitary activity, and what it asks for is a silence, a space, a setting, a place. Such

places suggest themselves, sudden oases with the promise of sustenance and temporary shelter. I have been
lucky in the oases I have stumbled on, some of them
preserved in writing, some of them in this book.

Much of what I have written, in poetry and in prose,
has had to do with place — with the interactions
between places and the people who live in them, with
what geographers call land-life relations. These vary
enormously, from country to country, from landscape
to language. For me, living in a place means deciphering
it, reading its omens, finding out how and why it
moves, feeling my way into its moods and its rituals.
All places are microcosms: the story of a single village
is in a sense the history of the universe. In a shifting,
changing world like the one we presently inhabit, the
houses we live in become our personal oases, small
worlds we are able to shape according to our lights,
shelters in every sense of the word.

Such oases, however, I have looked on as resting
places only, places eventually to move on from. The
one enduring oasis in my life has been my writing table,
which I set up wherever I find myself. I quote the Cuban
writer Guillermo Cabrera Infante, whose writing I revere:
There is an island of the present, and that is writing . . .
That island is my eternal island, the only kingdom I really
owe allegiance to, the only country I inhabit, the house
I live in, the house of words, the country of writing, the
kingdom of language.

Alastair Reid
May, 1997

Digging Up Scotland

I have a friend in Scotland, a painter, who still lives in the fishing town he was born in, grew up in, went to school in, was married in, raised his children in, works in, and clearly intends to die in. I look on him with uncomprehending awe, for although I had much the same origins that he had, born and sprouting in rural Scotland, close to the sea, living more by the agrarian round than by outside time, I had in my head from an early age the firm notion of leaving, long before I knew why or how. Even less did I realize then that I would come to restless rest in a whole slew of places, countries, and languages — the shifting opposite of my rooted friend. Walking with him through his parish, I am aware that the buildings and trees are as familiar to him as his own fingernails; that the people he throws a passing word to he has known, in all their changings, over a span of some fifty years; that he has surrounding him his own history and the history of the place, in memory and image, in language and stone; that his past is ever present to him, whereas my own is lost, shed. He has made his peace with place in a way that to me is, if not unimaginable, at least by now beyond me.

I spent a part of the summer of 1980 digging up

Scotland and to some extent coming to terms with it, for although I have gone back to it at odd intervals since I first left it, I have always looked on it more as past than as present. My childhood is enclosed, encapsulated in it somewhere, but the threads that connect me to it have long been ravelled. When I return, however, I realize that the place exists spinally in my life, as a kind of yardstick against which I measure myself through time — a setting against which I can assess more clearly the changes that have taken place in me, and in it. When I go back, I am always trying on the country to see if it still fits, or fits better than it did. In one sense, the place is as comfortable to me as old clothes; in another, it is a suit that did not fit me easily from the beginning.

Still, the landscapes of childhood are irreplaceable, since they have been the backdrops for so many epiphanies, so many realizations. I am acutely aware, in Scotland, of how certain moods of the day will put me suddenly on a sharp edge of attention. They have occurred before, and I experience a time warp, past and present in one, with an intense physicality. That double vision is enough to draw anyone back anywhere, for it is what gives us, acutely, the experience of living *through* time, rather than simply living *in* time. People's faces change when they begin to say 'I once went back to . . .' Something is happening to them; some rich realization, the thrill of retrieval that pervades Nabokov's writing, past and present in one. Places provide these realizations more readily than people do: places have longer lives, for one thing, and they weather in less unpredictable ways. Places are the incarnations of a modus vivendi and the repositories of memory, and so always remain accessible to their own children; but they make very different demands on their inhabitants. In Scotland, the sense of place is strong; when I had left that attachment behind me, I had a loose curiosity about new places, and I still spark up at the notion of going somewhere I have never been to before.

Nevertheless (a favourite Scottish qualification), places embody a consensus of attitudes; and while I lived in a cheerful harmony with the places I grew up in, as places, I did not feel one with them. The natural world and the human world separated early for me. I felt them to be somehow in contradiction. The Scottish landscape — misty, muted, in constant flux and shift — intrudes its presence in the form of endlessly changing weather; the Scottish character, eroded by a bitter history and a stony morality, and perhaps in reaction to the changing turbulence of weather, subscribes to illusions of permanence, of durability, asking for a kind of submission, an obedience. I felt, from the beginning, exhilarated by the first, fettered by the second. Tramps used to stop at our house, men of the road, begging a cup of tea or an old shirt, and in my mind I was always ready to leave with them, because between Scotland and myself I saw trouble ahead.

When I go back to Scotland, I gravitate mostly to the East Neuk of Fife, that richly farmed promontory jutting into the North Sea to the northeast of Edinburgh, specifically to the town of St Andrews, a well-worn place that has persisted in my memory from the time I first went there, a very young student at a very ancient university. I have come and gone at intervals over some thirty years, and St Andrews has changed less in that time than any other place I can think of. It is a singular place, with an aura all its own. For a start, it has a setting unfailingly beautiful to behold in any weather — the curve of St Andrews Bay sweeping in from the estuary of the River Eden across the washed expanse of the West Sands, backed by the windy green of the golf courses, to the town itself, spired, castled, and cathedraled, punctuated by irregular bells, cloistered and grave, with grey stone roofed in slate or red tile, kempt ruins and a tidy harbour, the town backed by green and gold fields with their stands of ancient trees. If it has the air of a museum, that is no wonder, for it sits placidly on top of a horrendous past. From the twelfth century on, it was in effect the ecclesiastical capital of Scotland, but the Reformation spelled its downfall: its vast cathedral was sacked, and by the seventeen-hundreds the place had gone into a sad decline. Its history looms rather grimly, not just in the carefully tended ruins of castle and cathedral but in the well-walked streets; inset in the cobblestones at the entrance to St Salvator's College quadrangle are the initials 'P.H.', for Patrick Hamilton, who was burned as a martyr on that spot in 1528; students acquire the superstition of never treading on the initials. With such a weighty past so tangibly present; the townspeople assume the air and manner of custodians, making themselves as comfortable and inconspicuous as they can among the ruins, and turning up their noses at the transients — the students, the golfers, the summer visitors. Yet, as in all such situations, it is the transients who sustain the place, who flock into it, year in, year out, to the present-day shrines of the university and the golf courses.

The date of the founding of the University of St Andrews is given, variously, as 1411 or 1412: the ambiguity arises from the fact that in fifteenth-century Scotland the year began on March 25, and the group of scholars who founded the institution received their charter in February of that dubious year. Such matters are the stuff of serious controversy in St Andrews. As students, we felt admitted to a venerable presence, even if the curriculum appeared to have undergone only minimal alteration since 1411. A kind of wise mist enveloped the place, and it seemed that we could not help absorbing it, unwittingly. The professors lectured into space, in an academic trance; we took notes, or borrowed them; the year's work culminated in a series of written examinations on set texts, which a couple of weeks of intense immersion, combined with native cunning and a swift pen, could take care of. What that serious, gravid atmosphere did was to make the present shine, in contradistinction to the past. Tacitly and instinctively, we relished the place more than the dead did or could, and we felt something like an obligation to fly in the face of the doleful past. The green woods and the sea surrounded us, the library, and an ocean of time. When I left St Andrews to go into the Navy in the Second World War, the place, over my shoulder, took on a never-never aura — not simply the never-neverness of college years but as contrast to the troubled state of the times. It appeared to me, in that regard, somewhat unreal.

In its human dimension, St Andrews embodied the Scotland I chose to leave behind me. The spirit of Calvin, far from dead, stalked the countryside, ever present in a pinched wariness, a wringing of the hands. We were taught to expect the worst — miserable sinners, we could not expect more. A rueful doom ruffles the Scottish spirit. It takes various spoken forms. That summer, a man in Edinburgh said to me, 'See you tomorrow, if we're spared,' bringing me to a horrified standstill. 'Could be worse' is a regular verbal accolade; and that impassioned cry from the Scottish spirit 'It's no' right!' declares drastically that *nothing* is right, nothing will ever be right — a cry of doom. Once at an international rugby match between Scotland and England in which the Scots, expected to win comfortably, doggedly snatched defeat from the jaws of victory, a friend of mine noticed two fans unroll a carefully prepared, hand-stitched banner bearing the legend 'WE WUZ ROBBED'. The wariness is deep-rooted. I prize the encounter I once had with a local woman on the edge of St Andrews, on a heady spring day. I exclaimed my pleasure in the day, at which she darkened and muttered, 'We'll pay for it, we'll pay for it' — a poem in itself.

And my father, who gleefully collected nuggets of utterance, often told of an old parishioner of his who, in the course of a meeting, rose to his feet and declared, 'Oh, no, Mr Reid. We've *tried* change, and we know it doesn't work.' I noticed on a bus I caught in St Andrews on my last visit, a sign that read 'PLEASE LOWER YOUR HEAD' — a piece of practical advice that had, for me, immediate Calvinist overtones.

Some of that girn and grumble lingers on in the Scots. The choice is to succumb to it or to struggle energetically against it. Or, of course, to leave it behind — the woe and the drear weather — and begin again in kinder climates. What Calvin ingrained in the Scottish spirit was an enduring dualism. 'The Strange Case of Dr Jekyll and Mr Hyde' is the quintessential Scottish novel. (The mysterious elixir of transformation is simply whisky, which quite often turns soft-spoken Scots into ranting madmen. Mr Hyde lurks in these silent depths.) Virtue had to be achieved at the expense of the flesh and the physical world, in which we were always being judged and found wanting — the world, it seemed, had a vast, invisible scoreboard that gave no marks for virtue but buzzed mercilessly at miscreants. It buzzed for me. It buzzed for me and for Kathleen, one of my sisters, so regularly that we became renegades, outwitting the system when we could. In St Andrews, that dire outlook regularly took the form of an audible sniff of disapproval.

I was born in rural Scotland, in Galloway, in the warm southwest, a gentle, kindly beginning, for we were bound by the rhythms of the soil, always out-doors, helping at neighbouring farms, haunting small harbours, looking after animals, or romping in the oat and barley fields that lay between our house and the sea. My father was a country minister, my mother a doctor. Summers, we shifted to the island of Arran: fish, mountains, and green fields. My father's parish had upward of seven hundred souls, in the village and on the surrounding farms, and, as often as not, my parents' stipends would come in the form of oats, potatoes, eggs, and game. When my father, from the pulpit, read of 'a land flowing with milk and honey', I was overcome by the beauty of the image, and had no doubt at all that he was talking about where we lived, for one of my chores was to fetch from the rich-smelling creamery across the fields a pitcher of milk still warm from the evening milking; the honey my father drew, with our wary help, from the hive at the end of the garden. When we eventually left Galloway for the flintier east, a glass closed over that time, that landscape. We had left the garden behind, and how it glowed, over our shoulders, how it shines!

The peopled world, as I grew into it from then on, seemed to me to take the form of an intricate network of rules designed to curb any spontaneous outbreak of joy or pleasure. The black cloud of Calvin that still hung over the Scottish spirit warned us from the beginning that our very existence was somehow unfortunate, gratuitous; that to be conspicuous through anything other than self-effacing virtue amounted to anarchy.

A God-fearing people — but the emphasis lay on the fearing. When I first took my son to Scotland, he asked me after only a few days, 'Papa, why are the people always saying they are sorry? What are they sorry about?' About their very existences, for they were forever cleaning and tidying, as though to remove all trace of their presence, as though bent on attaining anonymity. Nothing short of submission was expected. It seemed to me that the human world ran on a kind of moral economics, entirely preoccupied with judging and keeping score, while in the natural world I saw harmonies everywhere, I saw flux and change, but I saw no sharp duality. The two worlds were out of key.

A college friend of mine who later practised as a psychiatrist in Edinburgh was fond of saying that if Freud had known anything about Scotland he would have left Vienna like an arrow and taken on the whole population as a collective patient, to treat the national neurosis, the compulsive-obsessive rigidity that permeates its population. Yet as I look back on my childhood's cast of characters I am always amazed at what wild eccentricities the society accommodated, given its stern centre — what aberrant madnesses it managed to domesticate. It did so by marking out certain wilder souls as 'characters', thereby banishing them to glass bubbles of their own, and rendering them harmless. When I bring some of them to mind now — Pim the Poacher, who tracked down empty bottles all over the countryside and filled his cottage with them, all but one small room; Sober John, who read aloud from old newspapers in the marketplace — I realize that the people of the town unwittingly kept these poor souls safe by wrapping them in kindness. (A sort of impartial kindness prevails in Scotland, keeping stronger emotions in check — the kindness that takes the form of an immediate cup of tea for the distressed.) But the turning of certain individuals into 'characters' was also used to take care of dissident prophets and critics — anybody who threatened the unanimous surface of things. Similarly, at the University of St Andrews, dissenting students, if heard at all, were listened to with a tolerant, kindly half smile. ('Thank you. And now shall we return to the text?') Such a society must inevitably generate renegades, and Scotland has always done so, in droves — those renegades who turn up all over the world, not just as ship's engineers but in almost every outpost of civilization, where the cardinal Scottish virtue of self-sufficiency stands them in good stead.

There is also, I think, a geographical explanation for the steady exodus of the Scots over the years from their wizened little country. Scotland is an outpost — the end of the line. It is fastened to England, true, but not by any affection. The union — first of the Scottish and English crowns, in 1603, and then of Parliaments, in 1707 — created an entity, Great Britain, that has never really taken, in any deep sense. To the native fury of the Scots, the English refer to everything as English rather than British, and the fact that London, the capital, lies to the south is a constant source of irritation. The Scots' resentment of the English is aggravated by the fact that the English appear not to resent them back but treat Scotland as a remote region, whereas it remains, culturally, a separate country. But the sense of being on the receiving end, of living in a country that does not have much of a hand in its own destiny, causes a lot of Scottish eyes to narrow and turn to the horizon, and sends a lot of Scots in unlikely directions, the homeland a far green, rainy blur in their memory.

I had no such coherent notions, however, when I made up my mind to leave, for I must have been no more than seven at the time. Nor was it a decision as much as a bright possibility I kept in my head. We had been visited by a remote uncle, Willie Darling, who had gone to live in Christmas Island as a consulting engineer, and who spent his week with us illuminating that place with endless stories, pulling creased photographs from his wallet, reciting the names of exotic fruits as we struggled through our salt porridge. What dawned on me then, piercingly, was that ways of living, ways of thinking were *human* constructs, that they could, and did, vary wildly, that the imperatives the Scots had accepted were by no means absolute imperatives (except for them), that the outside world must contain a vast anthology of ways of being, like alternative solutions to a fundamental problem. As that relization took root in me, I was already distancing myself from Scotland — at least, from its more forbidding aspects. I had no idea at all about where I wanted to go, or how, or anything like that — only that I would. And I did.

St Andrews turned out to be my point of departure. I

left it after a brief first year to go into the Navy, and by the time I got back, after the end of the Second World War, I had seen the Mediterranean, the Red Sea, the Indian Ocean, and enough ports of call, enough human variety, to make St Andrews seem small and querulous. Yet the allure still hung over it, and I felt it still — felt the place to be, especially in the wake of the war years, something of an oasis. I have come and gone countless times since, returning, perhaps, because its citizens can be relied on to maintain it in as much the same order as is humanly possible. (In every town in Scotland, you will find houses occupied by near-invisible people whose sole function seems to be to maintain the house and garden in immaculate condition, as unobtrusively as they can. In New Galloway once, I watched a woman scrubbing the public sidewalk in front of her house with soap and water on two occasions during the day. She may have done it oftener, but I did not feel like extending my vigil.) The presence of the university and the golfing shrines has allowed St Andrews to preserve a kind of feudal structure: the university, being residential, houses and feeds its students, administers and staffs itself, and so provides a pyramid of work for the town, as does golf, whose faithful pilgrims keep hotels, caddies, and sellers of repainted golf balls in business. Others retire there, to its Peter Pan-like permanence, bringing their savings with them. As a result, the place has a bookish, well-to-do air, a kind of leisured aloofness this side of smug. I liked to imagine the wide cobbled centre of Market Street set with tables with red-checked tablecloths, between the Star Hotel and the Cross Keys, crisscrossed with singing waiters — Italians or, better, Brazilians, carrying laden trays, samba-ing, animating the place, rescuing it from its prim residents, forever hurrying home close to the old stone walls, eyes down, like nuns.

When the war and the University of St Andrews were behind me, I did begin to live what looks in retrospect like a very itinerant existence. But there is a certain obfuscatory confusion in the vocabulary: people used to ask me why I travelled so much, and I used to say emphatically that I did not in fact travel any more than was essential — what I did was live in a number of different places, a number of different countries, a number of different languages. Writing is about the most portable profession there is, yet sometimes it seemed to me that I was bent on proving this to be so by turning my curiosity into a kind of imperative to go off and write about places that had whetted my interest. I grew used to being a foreigner, but I chose to see it as a positive condition, as opposed to that of the tourist and the exile, who are connected by an elastic thread to somewhere else, who talk of 'going home' — a thing I never did. Disclaiming my roots, I elected instead not rootlessness, since that implies a lack, an unanchored attention, but a deliberate, chosen strangeness. I felt the whole notion of roots to be something of a distorting metaphor, applicable only in certain rural contexts, like the village I began in. What I was replacing a sense of roots with, I felt, was a deliberate adaptability. I became enmeshed in the places I lived in. The absorbing present seemed to me all there was, and I acquired a kind of windshield wiper attached to my attention, clearing each day of its antecedents.

It was at this point, in the early fifties, that I stumbled on Spain — not by design, since I knew not a word of the language, or by any particular impulse the other side of sheer curiosity. From my first chance landing there, I was drawn in by a certain human rhythm, a temper that, the longer I lived there, I felt to be an antidote to my frowned-on beginnings, to the earlier wringing of hands. There is a frank humanity to Spaniards that makes them accepting of, perhaps even delighted by, their own paradoxical natures. Gravity gives way to gaiety, fatefulness is leavened by a vivid sense of the present. The people in the village we lived in in Spain had a way of standing on their own ground, unperturbed, unafraid, 'listening to themselves living', as Gerald Brenan put it. They all seemed to me to be Don Quixote and Sancho Panza in one. They were comfortable occupying their own skins. They had achieved human imperviousness. V.S. Pritchett once wrote of 'the Spanish gift for discovering every day how much less of everything, material, intellectual, and spiritual, one can live on' — a quality that appealed to me. And as I moved into the language more and more, I felt altered by it. To enter another language is to assume much more than a vocabulary and a manner; it is to assume a whole implied way of being. In English, if

I get angry I tend to become tall, thin, tight-lipped; in Spanish, I spray anger around the room in word showers. Spanish, as a language, demands much more projection than English does. Hands and body become parts of speech. And then, of course, I began to read, discovering a whole abundance of literature that had been nothing more than a vague rumour in my mind. Spanish is quite an easy language to enter on the kitchen, or shopping, level. Beyond that, it grows as complex and subtle, in shading and tone, as any language does in its upper reaches. When I first met Spanish writers, I felt infinitely foolish at being able to utter no more than rudimentary observations, and I burrowed into the books they gave me, occasionally translating a poem, out of nothing more than zest. Translating was something that came to intrude more and more into my life, not so much out of intention as out of reading enthusiasm. But I felt in those first years in Spain that I was growing another self, separate and differently articulate. That experience was liberating, just as my first arrival in the United States had been — liberating in its openness and fluidity, as it is to all British people except those who cling excruciatingly to their meticulous, class-ridden origins.

I would go back to Scotland now and then, mostly in passing. It had receded in my attention, and I gave no thought to returning other than to reattach, in a fairly spectral sense, my irregular thread to the web of family. The point of going *back*, as I still said then, seemed an ever-diminishing one. People from my father's village, staunch citizens of St Andrews, members of my family, even, would fix me with a wary eye and say, 'You've been Away.' I could feel the capital A of 'Away' as a dismissal, a deliberate uninterest, and I conditioned myself to listen to the running account of local woes that followed. I would hardly have thought of referring to those occasions as joyous homecomings, although they had their revelations, mostly in the wet, soft, weather-stained landscape. They were nods in the direction of my origins, not much more. Scotland had become one of a number of countries with which I was comfortably familiar. I came across a poem by the Mexican poet José Emilio Pacheco, while I was translating a book of his, that so coincided with a poem I might myself have written that while I was translating it I felt I was writing the original. Here is my version:

I do not love my country. Its abstract splendour
is beyond my grasp.
But (although it sounds bad) I would give my life
for ten places in it, for certain people,
seaports, pinewoods, castles,
a run-down city, grey, grotesque,
various figures from its history,
mountains (and three or four rivers).

It was not long ago that my friend John Coleman pointed out to me the Spanish word *escueto*, deriving from the Latin *scotus*, a Scot. In present Spanish usage, it means 'spare', 'undecorated', 'stark'; but when we eventually looked it up in Coromina' etymological dictionary we found that Coromina had an extensive commentary on it, remarking at one point: '[the word] seems to have been applied to men who travelled freely, impelled by the practice of going on pilgrimages, very common among the Scots'; and he gives the meanings of 'free', 'uncomplicated', 'unencumbered', and 'without luggage'. The pilgrims obviously travelled light, probably with a small sack of oatmeal for sustenance. The word absorbed me, for it is clearly a *Spanish* notion, or translation, of the Scottish character — a view from outside, which chooses to interpret Scottish frugality as a freedom rather than a restraint. It was just the word for the transition I was then making. In Scotland, I had felt cumbered; in Spain, I was learning to be *escueto*, unencumbered.

*

In July of 1980, I returned to Scotland with a more specific purpose than I had had on innumerable previous visits: namely, to meet certain friends and dig up a small plastic box — a time capsule — we had buried there some nine years before.

*

By an accident of circumstance, I brought up my son, Jasper, by myself from roughly his fourth birthday on.

Our existence together continued itinerant — houses, countries, schools strung on it like beads on a chain. We invented a way of life that could not have a design to it, for we had no points of reference. At certain times, pretexts for moving somewhere else arrived, and we grew to accept these as omens. Spanish was Jasper's first language. Born in Madrid on August 9, 1959, he missed by about seven babies being the two-millionth inhabitant of Madrid, whose population now exceeds three and a half million. We rented an old house in Palma de Mallorca from Anthony Kerrigan, the translator — a house in which Gertrude Stein had spent a winter, we all later discovered, a steep, cool old house with a persimmon tree, close to a *parvulario*, where Jasper first went to school, in a blue smock, as Spanish children all did then. Waiting for him at the end of the day, I would hear fluting Spanish voices telling alphabets and numbers, an awe of first school in their voices. We moved for a year to New York, where I would walk Jasper to school in Greenwich Village and gain a new sense of the city through his eyes. But my father had been seriously ill, and though he had recovered, I had the feeling of wanting to be within range of him, so we sailed to London, and eventually came to rest in a houseboat on the Thames, moored with a colony of other boats along Chelsea Reach. There we floated for the next three years. Jasper walked to a Chelsea school along the Embankment, and would report sightings from the murky Thames — once a dead pig, floating trotters up. We took the train to Scotland sometimes — that northward transition in which the towns gradually shed decoration and grow starker, stonier, the landscape less peopled. The boat felt to us like a good compromise — we could in theory cast off, though our boat, an eighty-foot Thames barge, would, once out of its mud bed, have gone wallowing down in midriver.

Flist, we called the boat — a Scottish word that means a flash of lightning, of wit, a spark. Many friends came to visit, some of them out of sheer watery curiosity. The boat rose and fell on the tide twice a day, and, with visitors, we would wait for the moment when it shivered afloat, for they would stop, look into their drinks, look around as though they had been nudged by something inexplicable. I was translating some of the work of Pablo Neruda at the time, and when he came to London he took our boat in with a crow of delight and ensconced himself there. He held his birthday party on the boat, a materializing of Chileans, and we had to fish from the river a Ukrainian poet, turned to mudman on our stern. Neruda surprised me on that occasion by insisting that the company return at noon the following day, without fail — not exactly a normal English social procedure. As they straggled in, he handed each one a diplomatic glass of Chilean wine, and the party began all over again. At one point, Neruda took me aside. 'Alastair, you must understand, in your country people telephone, probably, to apologize for something they said or did; but we Chileans, we have learned to forgive ourselves everything, everything.' I felt he was giving me cultural absolution.

The existence of the houseboat fleet was always being threatened by some authority: in the eyes of houseowners and solid citizens, there was something raffish, gypsylike, about our floating community, and we held occasional impassioned meetings, vociferously bent on repelling boarders. Yet on weekday mornings from certain hatches would emerge some of our number, bowler-hatted and umbrellaed, bound for the City. Jasper and I became enmeshed in the life of the river, however, and lived as though with our backs to London.

*

I often wondered about our shifting, our moving, and would sometimes bring it up with Jasper, obliquely, at odd moments. I worried about its effect on him, but the signs were that he travelled well. He felt no particular fear about changing places, and instead had become adept at taking on languages and mannerisms. Moving had sharpened his memory, and he would astonish me at times by his recall. He could evoke sounds, atmospheres, houses in precise detail. If I had told him we were going to Bangkok for a while, he would have immediately looked it up in the atlas, without alarm. I had to remember that in one sense he looked on places like London and Scotland and New York as foreign and strange, familiar though they were to me;

but strangeness did not carry the aura of alarm to him — more the sense of another language, another way of being. I would concern myself with *his* feeling of rootlessness, only to realize that for him roots had little meaning. Not belonging to any one place, to any one context, he was in a sense afloat, and felt free to explore, to choose, to fit in or not — a freedom that in the long run made for a cool view. He did — and, I think, does — have a more intense sense of himself in Spain than in any other country. I had bought a small mountain retreat there in the early sixties, and although we did not go back to it with any calculable regularity, I saw how he lightened up whenever we did go. It was the only continuing past he had, and the villagers never failed to tell him how much he had grown, providing in general the trappings of childhood that our travelling life otherwise denied him. The house in Spain, however ghostly and remote it seemed to us from afar, served as the only fixed point in our existence. It was there that we took what we wanted to save — a kind of filing cabinet containing the keepsakes from other lives.

Our wandering life did impose certain restrictions: we could not, for example, have pets, because we moved in and out of the United Kingdom with such unpredictable regularity that the obligatory quarantine would have made them seem like children at boarding school. We had a more Hispanic attitude toward animals, looking on them as semidomestic creatures, whereas many of the English clearly prefer them to their fellows.

*

Inevitably — although there was nothing really inevitable about it — we moved. An invitation winged in to the houseboat one day from Antioch College, in Yellow Springs, Ohio (hard to find in the atlas), to teach for a year, and I accepted. We sold Flist, with many regrets and backward looks, and eventually shifted ourselves to a landscape new to both of us. The year was 1969, and the campus teemed and seethed; Kent State lay only two hundred miles away. Heralds came back from Woodstock with dirty, shining faces; no argument that year was less than elemental. At Antioch, we formed friendships that have lasted both vividly and ubiquitously; it was a year of fire, of passionate rethinking. Jasper trudged to a Yellow Springs school, and grew another American self, tempered by occasional nostalgic conversations and leavened by *The Whole Earth Catalog*, the handbook of the times. We had little idea of where we were going to go next, except to Scotland to visit my father, who was going to be eighty. So when the year ended we flew to Paris on a charter plane full of Antioch students chattering like missionaries, and wended our way north. To my relief, Jasper looked on Scotland as something of a comic opera, and I got glimpses of it through his eyes. He found its formality odd and stilted; he endured conversations that might have been scripted in stone. In a certain sense, he acknowledged it as my point of origin, but he made it clear that it was not his by suddenly speaking to me in Spanish in an overstuffed drawing room, out of pure mischief.

That summer of 1970, after spending some days with my father in the douce green Border hills, we took a spontaneous trip to St Andrews. I cannot quite remember how or when the thought occurred to us, but then, all at once, on whim, we decided to spend the year there. I had some long, slow work to do, and St Andrews boasted, besides its antiquated university, a venerable Georgian-fronted school called Madras College. On Market Street, I went into a solicitor's office peopled by gnomes and crones, and found that a house I had long known by sight was for rent — a house called Pilmour Cottage, not a cottage at all but an expansive country house, standing all by itself, about a mile from the centre of town, in a conspicuous clump of elm, oak, and sycamore trees, screened by an umbrella of resident crows, and facing the sea, some five hundred yards across the golf courses. It looked across at the estuary of the River Eden, on the other side of which lay Leuchars Aerodrome, where I had first taken flying lessons, with the University Air Squadron, during the war, and which had later gone from being a Royal Air Force fighter station to the strategic importance of an advanced NATO interceptor base, manned by Phantoms and Lightnings, and consequently, I imagined, a prime nuclear target — an irony sharpened by those benign surroundings. I rented the house without a second's hesitation, and in no time we were lugging our worldly goods across a sand path that threaded through green golfing sward to take possession of Pilmour Cottage for the next year — about as vast an expanse of future as we allowed ourselves in those travelling years.

Of all the houses we rented, borrowed, occupied, Pilmour Cottage remains, in both Jasper's memory and mine, the warmest, the most ample. It had six bedrooms, a cavernous dining room with a long oak table fit for banquets, and a huge, encompassing kitchen, with a great stove like an altar, where we gathered to keep warm, and where we practised the breadmaking skills we had acquired at Antioch. The kitchen window looked northeast to sea across the golf courses, and had a window seat where we spent a lot of time gazing. Day in, day out, in all weathers (and Scotland can assemble a greater variety of weathers in a single day than any other country I can think of), there trudged across our kitchen vision an unending plod of golfers, heads bent against the wind or frozen in the concentrated attitudes of the game. Jasper, bicycling back from school, would often turn up with a golf ball or two he had found on the path. We looked across at the square stone bulk of the Royal and Ancient Clubhouse, Camelot to all golfers, and we flew kites on the Old Course, their Mecca. It seemed somehow sacrilegious to live on the fringes of a turf whose sacred blades of grass were often clipped and mailed across the world as holy relics and not play golf ourselves; but we never got beyond acquiring a putter, which we would sometimes wield on the empty greens toward sunset, and an old wood, with which we would occasionally drive the lost balls we had accumulated into the whin bushes, to be found over again. The golfers were part of the landscape, like moving tree stumps; but one spring morning we looked out amazed to see the whole course dotted with tartan-bonneted Japanese, who had made their exhausting pilgrimage to play there for one day, and who insisted on photographing us as typical natives.

I looked from my workroom across the expanses of grass, sand, sea, and sky, quite often at the expense of my work, so mesmerizing was that landscape. Wind-bare, sand-edged, with clumps of whin and marram punctuating the expanses of rough fescue grass, the landscape had clearly brought the game of golf into being. The Old Course at St Andrews has been both cradle and model; other golf courses can be seen as variations on its fundamental setting. The St Andrews golf courses, four of them in all, are grafted onto the town by way of clubhouses, golf shops, hotels, and wide-windowed bars — an enclosed world through which we passed on bicycles, still clinging to our immunity.

We settled into Pilmour Cottage as though we had lived there forever and would never move. All year long, a succession of friends came to stay, arriving sleepily off the morning train from London and opening their eyes wide when they saw where they were. We explored the countryside, we beachcombed, we sometimes even swam in the chilling North Sea. We wandered into the town and idled in bookstores, the stony town now brightened by the scarlet gowns of the students.

Jasper took to saying 'Aye!' and soon had the protective coloration of a working Fife accent. One afternoon, we opened the door to a young man named Jeffrey Lerner, an Antioch student whom we had not known in Yellow Springs but who was spending his junior year (improbably, to us) in St Andrews, reading Scottish history. We all had many friends and turns of mind in common, and Jeff ended up renting a room from us, since we had rooms to spare, even with visitors. The arrangement worked wonderfully well from the start, for I was able to make some necessary trips, leaving Jasper in Jeff's care. Jasper was eleven at the time, Jeff twenty-one and the right cast for a hero, and I felt considerably relieved to have Jeff as an attendant spirit. I went to Spain at the end of the year, briefly, to settle up some matters in the village and to see how the house was weathering. I shivered in the stone house there, bare feet on the tile floor. Scotland was warmer by far, in a winter so balmy that we never once saw snow and throughout which we continued to fly the kites we kept building — elaborate kites, which stood in the hall like ghost figures and which we flew to enormous heights, sometimes even using them to tow our bicycles. Jasper and his school friends took over the outdoors and the trees, tracked through the dunes, and mimicked the crows till they rose in tattered black clouds.

Coincidentally, 1971 was the year Britain changed from its clumsy ancestral coinage to the decimal system. The *Scotsman*, our daily source of Scottish illumination, bristled with angry letters, and on the day of transition

Market Street was dotted with dazed locals gazing at handfuls of glistening new change, holding up unfamiliar coins, shaking their heads, sure that the terrible innovation would not last. We hoarded the ponderous old pennies in a jar in the hall, and we had the feeling that the foundations were being shaken for once — that the past was, even in this everyday, metallic form, yielding to the present.

That year, August of 1970 until June of 1971, was the first I had spent in Scotland since I left it, and I found myself taking stock of it — as it, I imagined, was taking stock of me. The Hispanic world irredeemably alters one's notion of time, since it reacts instinctively, existentially, against the imposition of order from outside, particularly the order of the clock, and substitutes human time. Things take as long as they need to, and happen when they must. That had seeped into me sufficiently to make me intensely aware of the orderliness of St Andrews. Something was always chiming. Punctually at five-thirty in the evening, the streets emptied; shop locks clicked shut almost simultaneously up and down the street. It felt like a place that had taken care to deprive itself of surprises. Jeff, newly translated from the Antioch of the sixties, could not believe the receptive obedience of his fellow students. As we settled into St Andrews, the outside world grew hazy and remote. St Andrews had domesticated it, making things predictable, untroubled. Yet I felt that, once again, sitting in the middle of the landscape translating Spanish texts, I was more estranged than ever from the formalities of the place. The presence of Jasper and Jeff, bringing back separate, hilarious stories from school and university, set me sometimes to trying to explain Scotland to them, and in so doing I came to see how little I identified with it at any point. It was the year that *Monty Python* made its first appearance on British television, and in their eyes St Andrews felt like an endless rerun of the programmes.

In April, the Argentine writer Jorge Luis Borges came to visit, on his way to receive an honorary degree from Oxford University. Borges was much affected by being in Scotland, although his blindness denied him the sight of it. He would take walks with Jasper or Jeff, talking intently, and recite Scottish ballads to us round the kitchen table. During the week that Borges spent with us, the official census-taker arrived at our household. The British are most scrupulous about the census, and the census-taker sat himself down at the long dining-room table, calling us in one by one to record not only our existences but a dossier of ancestral detail. Borges; Maria Kodama, his Japanese-Argentine travelling companion; Jasper; Jeff — I have forgotten who else, but I was the only member of the household born in Scotland. As I showed the official out, he turned to me, scratching his head, and said, 'I think, Mr Reid, I'll just put you all down under "Floating Population".' He had a point.

My sister Kathleen lived in Cupar, some eight miles inland from us, and in the course of that year Jasper discovered relatives who until then had been only names to him. Kathleen had five children, who formed a rambunctious household — a family that in human energy far exceeded the sum of its parts, for it put out enough to light a small town. Jasper was astonished by his cousins. He gaped at the whole bewildering whirl of family connection. Our own family structure felt tame in comparison — ludicrously simple. The fact of his having been born in Spain made the others peer at him as though he might be an extraterrestrial. The astonishment was mutual, for my sister's children were voluble and full of questions. By now, however, Jasper had grown expert at being a Martian. His three nationalities — Spanish, British, and American — had made him a foreigner in every school class he sat in, and he wore his oddness quite jauntily. He was, I think, ahead of me.

An early spring brought greenness and soft air, carpets of daffodils surrounding the house, larks hanging invisibly over the golf course, disappeared into song. The days lengthened, and the golfers played late into the long twilight. We discussed building a tetrahedral kite, modelled on one with which Alexander Graham Bell had once lifted a man, and Jasper looked alarmed. He played cricket for the first time in his life, with a certain disbelief. I came one morning upon a grey heron standing in the driveway like an omen, and we gazed at each other for a full ten minutes. Swallows and swifts appeared, strafing the house all day.

It was on one of those spring evenings that we

decided, on the spur of the moment, to bury the time capsule. I cannot remember who raised the notion or why — it may easily have come from a book one of us had been reading, or simply from whim — but once we had the idea in our heads we scuttled about, gathering up elements of the place we felt to be worthy of encapsulation. We found an opaque plastic box with a tight-fitting lid in the kitchen cupboard, and we poured into it first the jarful of obsolete pennies and then the contents of a box in which we had kept all manner of foreign coins left over from various travels. We got together some photographs and letters, the local paper (the St Andrews *Citizen*, which we read assiduously every week), other miscellaneous documents, representative talismans that we turned up at short notice. We realized that we had to prepare a note to accompany the scrambled contents, and it was at that stage that Jeff pointed out that burying the box would be fairly absurd unless we expressed an intention to dig it up somewhere along the line. So, casting about for an arbitrary date sufficiently far off in time, we came up with Jasper's twenty-first birthday, August 9, 1980 — an occasion so unimaginably far away as to render us helpless with laughter, for then he came up to the height of the stove, and the thought of him tall and grave, with a deep voice, convulsed us all. We packed in the contents, signed our declaration of intent, made some notes on the day and on what we had just had for dinner, then sealed the lid on with epoxy glue. The twilight was deepening into owl-light when we went out bearing the box, a couple of spades, and a lantern lit for the occasion. It had begun to rain lightly as we crossed the front lawn and climbed over the wall into a clump of scrub and rough grass edging the golf course. We decided on that spot because it was public ground, and we wanted the place to be accessible when the time came. A small elm tree stood about twenty feet from the wall, so we chose it as our marker, measuring out an appropriate distance from it, which we all committed to memory, and set to digging. The box was duly buried and the soil restored — with unholy haste and an absence of ritual, because the rain was thickening and the lantern went out in a hiss. We hurried in to get dry, leaving the box behind us in the ground like a knot tied in the past to remind us of something.

Not long after that, a letter came inviting me to Mexico in the fall. It coincided with a vague plan I'd had of spending some time in Latin America, which Jasper had never seen, but with which I was becoming more and more involved, so, after Jasper and I talked about it, after he took a book on Mexico out of the school library and fixed Mexico for himself on his private map, I accepted. I had never raised the question of staying in Scotland, nor had he. Jeff was winding up his year, studying for final exams, making plans — first, to ship out on a French fishing boat, which he did from Lorient, in Brittany, and then to make his way back to Antioch, by way of our house in Spain. The end of spring was crowned by school sports day, the departure of students; my own work was almost finished. When Jeff left, the suspension in which we had lived all year was broken, and we found ourselves back in time. Our lease on Pilmour Cottage would soon be up, and I made plans to go to Spain on the way to Mexico, and once more assembled our worldly goods, dividing what to abandon from what to keep.

There were rituals of passage, leave-takings, last walks, backward looks. We had arrived in and gone from places so often, and seen so many people leave, that we were familiar with all the facets of departing. When the moment came, we took a long look over our shoulders at Pilmour Cottage from the Cupar Road, with a certain quick pang — the house across that low-lying landscape already half hidden in its own elms and pines, the crows hovering. Pilmour Cottage began to dwindle away in an odd kind of smoke. We had already forgotten the box in the ground.

*

For Jasper and me, the summer in Spain quickly became the present — a preoccupying present, because we were putting a new roof on the house there, sleeping, out of necessity, in the ilex forest, and catching up on village matters, changing languages again. Pilmour Cottage had gone into the archives. Certain appendages of it — a wooden spoon, a few golf balls, an etching of St Andrews someone had given us in farewell — joined the array of keepsakes in the Spanish house. Jasper sometimes mentioned Pilmour, already handling the memory like a memento, a token. We caught a boat from Barcelona to Venezuela in early fall and made our way to Mexico. Jasper attended an international school in Cuernavaca, learning, it seemed to me, not much more than the Mexican national anthem, but that indelibly. We spent some time in Mexico City with the exiled Spanish writer Max Aub, an old mentor of mine — and an inspiring presence, because he was forever inventing imaginary writers, writing their works, and then entering into controversy with them. Late in the year, we took a freighter from Tampico to Buenos Aires, stopping, apparently at the captain's whim, along the South American coast. It was almost Christmas by the time we reached Buenos Aires — the beginning of summer there, which meant that all schools were closed. So during our time there and, later, in Chile — the hopeful Chile of Allende, before things began to fray away — Jasper went schoolless, but he was never at loose ends, for the Chile of those days made St Andrews (or would have, if we had ever thought of it) more like an invention of ours, a place we had once dreamed up, a place where nothing happened, as different from Chile as was imaginable.

After that long wander, we came to rest in London. It seemed to me imperative that, with such patchwork schooling, Jasper should finish up within one school system, with a semblance of order to it. So he went to school in Highgate and came to terms with England.

Apart from irregular sallies to Spain, we stayed put for four years.

Jeff, meanwhile, had finished up at Antioch, had married Nora Newcombe, a redheaded and warm-witted Canadian girl, who had visited us at Pilmour, and who was doing a PhD in psychology at Harvard. We did not see them for a long while, but we wrote when it seemed unforgivable not to. Then the work Jeff was doing — a PhD thesis on the shifting attitudes toward bereavement in the course and aftermath of the First World War — brought them to London one summer, and we fell excitedly to filling in the missing time. With Nora and Jeff an ease of connection had existed from the very beginning, where we never tired of talking and noticing. The connection they had with Jasper was particularly important in my eyes, and I knew that it was in theirs: they paced his growing, their persistence as recurring friends a matter of great import to him, since he always had so many things to tell them, to ask them, when we met up. We had occasional, surreal, smokily distant conversations about Scotland; but we did not talk about the box.

I went to Scotland off and on from London. My parents grew frailer; my mother died, as emphatically as she had lived; and my father moved between the houses of two of my sisters, where I would go to visit him. On one of these visits, while he was living with Kathleen, I drove over to Pilmour Cottage, took a mooning walk around the house and climbed over the wall to the vicinity of the elm tree. The ground had a thick undergrowth, but I could still feel, at the appropriate distance from the tree as I calculated it, a recognizable hollow, a comfortable sag in the ground.

*

From 1970, five years passed without my coming to the United States — an unimaginable hiatus, for I had been in this country almost every year, or some part of it, since I first came at the end of the forties. I'm not sure now why that hiatus developed, except that we were more European-minded at the time, and that in London friends from New York were always passing through, giving us the illusion of being in touch. I was working, also, through another long scrabble of translation, and I was caught up in the flurry of disaster that followed the coup in Chile — Chileans arriving in London, anxieties of not knowing — and in the obvious withering away of Franco in Spain. In the summer of 1975, however, some pretext arose for my going to the United States, and I decided to take Jasper, since he had not seen any of his American relatives in a long time, let alone the landmarks he remembered. New York felt sunny after London — not literally but humanly. I warmed myself with friends I had not seen in too long. Londoners are scrupulous about one another's privacy, and New York seemed loose and luxurious after the primness of the London years. We did, however, spend those London years in Victoria, a neighbourhood that had become the headquarters of

Spaniards who had left Spain in those lean times to find work elsewhere in Europe, so I shopped in Spanish at the street market, kept up with the Spanish football scores, and would translate the odd will or document into English for Doña Angelina, who ran a Spanish boardinghouse close to where we lived, and who knew our Spanish village well.

The United States this time had as visibly liberating an effect on Jasper as it had had on me at first gasp. I could see him taking forgotten selves out of the closet and shaking the dust from them. From this vantage point, London seemed suddenly such a polite place — if anything, overcivilized. When I returned to it, in midsummer, it was with a surge of that extra energy I have always absorbed while visiting New York (though not necessarily while living in it). But I returned for a specific purpose; namely, to take my father back to the house he had lived in in the Borders, in order to give my sisters something of a break. Poor old man, he was already tired of his long existence, although he had bright moments. He rested at least half of each thick, green summer day, and again I found myself sitting, alone, in that shifting landscape, writing, wondering, while my father moved closer to dying, too tired, eventually, to say another word. He died as that summer mellowed into September, the way it does in Scotland.

*

Jasper finished school in London in 1977, and so we shuttered up the Victoria flat (which I had rented from Lesley, another sister of mine) and came to the United States again, I on my way to Costa Rica, Jasper to find himself a job for a year before going to college. I had been with him, mostly, for close to fourteen years, and there were moments at first when I would suddenly feel that it was time I got home, only to remember that there was no particular reason, no urgency. We were both relieved to separate, I think, for we needed our own lives, and Jasper seemed quite adept at running his. Time passed, comings and goings. Nora was appointed assistant professor of Psychology at Penn State, and she and Jeff moved there, Jeff still lugging his thesis with him. I went to Brazil, to England. When I got back to New York, Jasper announced to me that he had been accepted at Yale. We could think of nothing to do immediately but laugh our heads off.

On New Year's Day of 1980, the day before I left for Puerto Rico, we had a party at my apartment in Greenwich Village, for Jeff and Nora were in New York, Jasper had a job in the city over Christmas, and other friends were stopping by from various places. Sometime during the day, Jasper, Nora, Jeff, and I found ourselves sitting round the table practising writing '1980' on the white tabletop. It dawned on us all at the same moment, as though someone had tugged at the knot, that ahead, in summer, lay the box in the ground. We did our share of comic head-shaking and hand-wringing, in the Scottish manner, and then we drew ourselves up, Jasper taller now than we could ever have imagined, and took solemn vows to present ourselves in Scotland in August.

*

In mid-July, I prepared to leave New York, first for London, where I had to see friends, and then for Scotland, because I had not really been back since my father died. I had some work to do in Edinburgh, and I wanted to be sure of having a place to house the others if they turned up. There was a measure of doubt. I could not get hold of Nora and Jeff, who were somewhere in Philadelphia, and all I could do was leave them a message that I was going. Jasper was driving a taxicab in New York, and was rueful, in the way of students, about time and money. We considered for a moment postponing the disinterment until we were all more moneyed and more leisured, and horrified ourselves by the thought. So I left. I passed through London, took the train north once again, and landed in late July at Kathleen's house in Cupar, in the mainstream of a rained-out summer that was causing even the natives to grumble in disgust.

Kathleen and I have always shared an easy dimension. We forgave each other from an early age. She has a marked generosity of spirit, and is never still. To my astonishment, I found myself surrounded this time by great-nieces: my sister's two eldest daughters, Sheelagh and Gillian, had already had seven daughters between them, and there was a little army of knee-high girls whose names I had to learn. Sheelagh and Gillian had both married solicitors, both of whom worked in Cupar, for rival firms; Kathleen's husband, Charlie, was the bank manager. It all felt very dynastic to me, although at times it took on aspects of a Scottish soap opera.

In Scotland, the buying and selling of houses is generally managed through solicitors, and Sheelagh's husband, George McQuitty, handled such matters with considerable dash. In the course of doing so, he had acquired for himself and his family an imposing pile called Seggie House, built before 1900 for the factor of the paper mill at Guardbridge, four miles from St Andrews along the Cupar Road. The sprawling house had a separate apartment, which I rented from George and Sheelagh. I had known the house under previous owners, but not as it now was, an anthill of activity. It had ample grounds and stands of trees, it had lawns, it had a huge, walled vegetable garden with a grape-bearing greenhouse, and it even had a tower, with a view of the Eden estuary and the surrounding countryside.

George, stocky, soft-spoken, has a quiet, burning energy, and at Seggie he was turning it to account. From a window, I would see him drive in at the end of a day, in a business suit and tie, and not five minutes later a chain saw or a mower would start up: George, in blue jeans, transformed into farmer. They kept pigs, chickens, geese, and three goats. George felled trees, turned hay, fed animals, rescued children. Everything we ate seemed to come from Seggie; what we left went back to the pigs. Sheelagh, in almost direct contrast to George, has such a vivid electricity to her that she seems to move and talk twice as fast as anyone else, and then she falls back into the repose of a smile. The girls descended in size from Jane, who, rusty-haired and serious, knew everything about *Dallas*; through Kate, moonier and more reticent; and Sara, four, with a piercingly unabashed curiosity; to Kirsty, five months old, who sat on the kitchen table and seemed to be fed by everybody. I never knew who was in the house — or, indeed, where anyone was — except at mealtimes, when they all magically materialized, as the food did. Sheelagh shot off somewhere to teach a class, to take a class, to exchange a child. The growl of the mower signalled that George was back. For me, in that humming establishment, writing felt like an indolent pastime.

I dawdled in Edinburgh — still alluring to me, a walking city. It did look dour, though, after New York. I went in to St Andrews, called on some friends, bumped into others. They all asked me what I was doing in Scotland. I told the story once, but not again, inventing some other pretext. It suddenly seemed a rather weird story. August arrived. July, according to some accounts, had been the wettest in three hundred years. I had to tell the story of the box to the children, who thought it terrific, except that they doubted

Jasper's existence, for they had never seen him to remember.

There is such a deep green to Scotland in midsummer; even in the drizzle, the greenness emerges, and much came back to me as I breathed that summer in. The countryside swelled with growing, and I sometimes drove through the small, neat villages of Fife: Balmullo, Ceres, Crail, Windygates — names my tongue knew well. Talking to George and Sheelagh, I found them cheerfully liberated from the glooms that still hung in my memory, although they were well aware of them. They also appeared relatively unperturbed about matters of money — a change from the frayed days I remembered, when it would have been unthinkable to buy anything without having the actual coin in hand, and when I once asked my father to show me a pound note and he had to go look for one, since he never carried money with him. But then Scotland had badly needed not a generation gap but a generation gulf, and Sheelagh and George certainly had as acute a sense of the world as anybody, brushing aside insularities by ignoring them. They lived a thoughtful rural life — one that was always being translated into activity. On some days, Seggie House seemed as strenuous to me as New York.

I spent Thursday, August 7, in Edinburgh, recording a broadcast for the BBC. I took a train back to Leuchars Junction, the nearest station to Seggie House, and when I got to the house Sheelagh met me in the hall. 'Your friends are in the kitchen,' she said over her shoulder on her way to feed the chickens. I went through, and there were Jeff and Nora, with children all over them. They had rented a small car and driven up from London. By judicious phone calls, they had traced me to Seggie, but their call had been answered by Mrs Trail, who helped Sheelagh keep the household back from chaos, and her directions had proved unintelligible. They had had to intuit their way. That same evening, a cable came from Jasper saying he was taking the night plane to London and would call the next morning. We sat in the kitchen and talked, the girls wandering down from sleep on some wild pretext ('I just wanted to ask Alastair something, honestly!'), not wanting to miss anything. Sheelagh filed Jeff and Nora away in some part of the house I don't think I had even seen. There was a thunderstorm that night, and in my sleep I heard the goats bleat.

Jasper called the next morning around breakfast time. He was in London with a friend of his from Yale. They were taking the train up, and, with a change in Edinburgh, would reach Leuchars Junction about eight that evening. Jeff and Nora, both goggle-eyed at being back in Fife, went off to explore St Andrews, suspending their disbelief. The girls were already enthusiastic about an obvious chance to stay up late. But we kept studiously clear of Pilmour Cottage, as I had done since I arrived. It was for the next day. We drove down at sunset to Leuchars Junction to meet the train, which ground in, salutarily late, and let out Jasper and his friend Allen Damon. We got them into the

Mini Jeff and Nora had rented, with some difficulty, for Allen turned out to be six feet five, and intricate human folding was required. We all ended up in the kitchen, eleven of us now, like an assembled freak show, for the sight of Sara standing beside Allen was comical. Jasper had a beard and looked tired. It occurs to me that I have not described Jasper — perhaps because there are for me so many of him, each separate self associated with a particular place, each distinct in my memory. By now, he is about the same height I am, just over six feet; physically, we do not look at all alike, except possibly around the eyes, but we have a wavelength and a language in common, which we fall into very easily. Sheelagh produced food as she always did — less, apparently, by cooking than by willing it into being. We sorted each other out, telling our separate stories, everyone surprised for a time at the presence of everyone else, everyone talking, a stew of accents. At some point, we made an agenda for the following day: we would wake early, dig up the box, bring it back to Seggie, and then make lunch, to which we had invited all the stray members of the voluminous family that seemed to be sprouting with the summer. George had already laid out a selection of spades, shovels, hoes, and picks, and the weather forecast promised a fair day, as they say in Fife.

*

Next morning, we began to materialize in the kitchen

about seven — Jasper and Allen last, jet-lagged. Over breakfast, we ordered the day. The five of us would go, taking Jane along with us. George might drop in later if we were not back. We folded ourselves into the Mini and set out for Pilmour Cottage.

There was a new way into Pilmour, past a practice green; a parking area had taken shape where our old imposing gateway had been. But as we shouldered our spades, trudged round the perimeter of bushes, and caught sight of the house, it all swam back, in a trance of time. The house was white and well kept, the grass juicy around it, the trees enveloping, the day, I am glad to say, dry, with a suggestion of sun. Golfers were already out; it was a Saturday morning. I had looked in on Mr Stewart, the present owner of Pilmour Cottage, at his store in St Andrews, to tell him sketchily what we would be doing, and he had been quite jovial about our return, promising us extra spades if we needed them. We stood by the wall for a while looking at the house, shifting it back and forth in our heads — all except Allen, who had never seen it before. A sometime golfer in Hawaii, where he came from, he gazed across the Old Course with a player's awe. The morning was warming, and we were in no hurry, except for young Jane, who could not wait to be astonished. So we turned away from the house and found the elm tree, now grown into an adult elm.

It was at this point that a hesitation set in. Jasper, given the privilege, paced off a certain distance from the tree perpendicular to the wall, dug in his heel, and reached for a spade. 'No!' Jeff was waving his arms wildly. 'You've forgotten. It was three arm spans from the tree.' And he started measuring off the spans. But whose arm spans, I asked him. Jasper's? He had been a lot smaller then. Besides, I told them both, I had been back to the site once, and what we had to feel for with our feet was a depression, a sag — as I began to do, in the thick tangle of undergrowth. We agreed, however, to start digging at Jasper's spot and then, if we did not find the box at once, to dig in the places that Jeff and I had picked out as more likely. Well, we did not find the box at once. We dug in a desultory way for about an hour, expecting with every spade thrust to feel a clunk of a kind, a plastic clunk. We found a teacup, unbroken, and a bent spoon. We talked about memory, leaning on our spades. Jeff and Jasper began to recreate the burying of the box, and even on that they began to diverge. Jasper didn't think that it had been raining that night, and hence surmised that the box must be buried deeper, about four feet down. I was sure of the rain, for I remembered the lantern going out. When we could not remember, we grew adamant. Nora and Allen went off to find some coffee, perhaps in the hope that, left to concentrate, we might clarify our collective memory. We did not. Jane pointed out where *she* would have buried a box, and she might well have been right, because although the presence of the house began to remind all three of us of innumerable details of the past, it did not tell us where to dig. A trance set in again for a moment. We dug more. I had broken ground where I thought the box was, although I admitted to feeling promising sags all over the place. My spade clanged against something — a buried can. Nora and Allen came back, and Nora told us about 'state-dependent memory', which she elaborated on at some length. It beat digging. Although the presence of Pilmour Cottage was activating our general recall, she explained, we would have to recover the precise mood and emotion surrounding the event to narrow down our memory. But these were nine years behind us now. (She recently sent me an article from the February issue of *American Psychologist* that told me a great deal about state-dependent memory. It is something I have experienced a lot, changing countries. When I go back to somewhere I have previously lived, I put my arms into the sleeves of the place at once, and find that I take on not just its timetable and its eating habits; I also experience moods heavy with dormant memory.) We laid out what we dug up, however, as methodically as archaeologists, and we soon had a fair array of objects — more spoons, broken crockery, medicine bottles gummy with mysterious resins, a child's tin toy from nurseries ago.

Then George turned up, having already been to his office and subsequently sawed up a felled tree. (Jeff had earlier suggested altering a road sign near Seggie from 'MEN WORKING' to 'GEORGE WORKING'.) George sized up the scene: we had already dug deepish holes at three points of a triangle of which each side was some eighteen feet long — so widely can memory wander.

He asked us a few brief questions, then proceeded to excavate a trench, clearing off the undergrowth with a few cuts of his spade, and digging cleanly down, the walls of his trench exquisitely perpendicular and sharp compared with our molelike burrowings. He made us all tired, but we dug, scraping our way, as it were, toward one another. We leaned on our spades whenever it was decently possible, and looked at one another. It was time to be at Seggie for lunch. Spades shouldered, we stumbled back to the car. My instep hurt.

The children, far from crestfallen, were glad to have their anticipation extenuated. Kathleen arrived, with Charlie, bluff, looking not older but more so, as Jasper said, and Gillian, Fiona, another niece, Roy, her husband — here the canvas gets a bit crowded. But we ate well — salmon that Charlie had caught and smoked, a ham we had dealt for with a neighbouring farmer, green abundance from the garden, raspberries that Kathleen had picked that morning. I sat on the step with Jeff a few moments. 'Has it occurred to you that this could have a lot of different endings?' he asked me. It had. The girls had put out on the front lawn a table with a white cloth, to receive the box. We looked at each other, gathered our spades, and got ready to clamber back into the car.

It was at this point that George had a brain wave. A doctor friend of his occasionally repaired electronic equipment, and had, he remembered, tinkered with a metal detector for a fellow who lived on the far side of Cupar. He was on the phone in a flash, and in no time we were speeding to pick up the machine — which had been acquired by its owner, George told me in the car, after his wife threw her wedding ring into a field during an argument. They had not, however, found the ring — an ill omen, I felt. Nor did the machine itself look capable of pinpointing our lost box. We stopped at Seggie to pick up children, for Kate and Sara would not be left out, and neither would anyone else, for that matter, except Charlie, who was already sensibly asleep under a newspaper. We arrived at the site this time like an army, aghast at the chaos we had already created in vain. Jeff and Nora had somehow disappeared, strayed. But we began to dig again while Jane combed the promised ground with the metal detector. After a few excited sorties, we abandoned it, having found that it could not detect even a pile of change we planted no more than six inches down.

George, fortified by lunch, dug off in a new direction. The children pestered us with questions, and we began to feel a little foolish, particularly when a man who was visiting Pilmour Cottage wandered over to the wall. He could not contain his curiosity any longer, he told me, and when I explained what we were doing he looked at me somewhat sorrowfully and wished me luck. The sun was out, the day had turned glorious, Jasper had turned twenty-one, and we had dug up a patch of ground about the size, it seemed to me, of a small midtown office. And where were Jeff and Nora? George, leaning on his spade, looked a bit worn. It was the thought of unproductive labour that was bothering him, I think. It was bothering me. The children had extended our collection of relics considerably, by bringing in odd golf balls and empty bottles from the undergrowth. I hoped they were not losing faith. The clink of golf clubs and the thud of golf balls punctuated the whole day steadily, as golfers, unperturbed by our gypsy encampment, cheerfully hacked their way home. As Kathleen was preparing to remove some children, at a sign of lengthening shadows, Nora and Jeff burst out of the undergrowth, carrying what looked to me like a ray gun with a set of stereo headphones attached. It was a metal detector that looked as if it might have a chance. Jeff wasted no time in beginning to comb the ground with it. Even George cheered up. Nora explained. They had driven into St Andrews and gone to hardware stores in the hope of renting a metal detector. An ironmonger in Market Street did not have one for rent or for sale — fortunately, for it would have cost about as much as a used car — but he remembered selling one last Christmas to a woman who lived on the far edge of town and whose daughter worked in Henderson's, the booksellers. They had tracked down the girl, got from her her mother's address, driven there, explained (I know not in what form) to the *dueña* of the metal detector — Mrs Brian, of Schoolbraids Road — and come away with it and more good wishes. At that point, Jeff whooped and jumped up and down, jabbing his finger at the ground. We dug deeper, for Jeff was still gesticulating. Another old can, but this one quite far down, giving us at least a glimmer of faith in the machine. As if to vary our luck we all took turns, we all jumped up and down, we found seven more rusted cans. Kathleen sagely decided to go back with the baby, but the other children were still glowing, so they stayed. George's face had lengthened like the shadows. Around that time, Jeff and I began passing the metal detector (Adastra, it was called) back and forth between the end of the trench George had dug when he first appeared and the elm tree — closer to the tree. No question, there was an unmistakable hum, a steady hum, a hum that seemed to cover the area of the box as we imagined it. We whistled over Jasper with his spade. He dug, again; again, a bump — and we were on the box. We all stopped. Jasper scraped away the last dirt with his hands, and there it was, less than two feet down, not much more than two feet from the tree. It was slightly split, clearly from the blow of a spade — probably George's first spade cast, we speculated later. We lifted it out carefully and laid it to one side. It was six-fifteen, a golden evening; even the golfers, however, were thinking of going in.

Hilariously, we pitched in to restore a semblance of order to the ground we had combed — with our fingers, it felt. We had to persuade Sara to save only the best of our recovered artifacts. The rest we reburied, leaving the ground as level as we could, to go back to undergrowth. We wound our way to the cars like Millet peasants — tools shouldered, children carried — bound for Seggie. It was going on twilight by the time we got there. We decided to wash off before we got to the box, for none of us were regular diggers and we had managed to cover ourselves with native earth. My instep hurt almost enough for me to limp, but not quite.

When we had assembled ourselves, we moved the box into the dining room and clustered around the table. I had grown curious about the contents, because I had only a vague memory of them. We began to remove them, one at a time. First, however, on top, lay the card we had added at the last minute, before we sealed the box. We read the text aloud. It was full of ironies. 'This chest,' it said starkly, 'containing treasure in coin and various souvenirs of the present moment in St Andrews in May 1971, is buried here by Jasper Reid, Jeff Lerner, and Alastair Reid, in a spot known to these three persons.' George smiled wanly. 'It is their intention to return on the ninth day of August, 1980, to meet and disinter the chest in one another's company, and to celebrate their survival with appropriate ceremony. Sunday, May 30, 1971, a hazy day with sea mist, rooks, curry, and kites.' And under that were the signatures, mine recognizably the same, Jeff's looking somewhat simplified, Jasper's in large, errant schoolboy handwriting.

We looked at one another. There we all were. We had survived even the digging.

The contents of the box, I am sorry to say, amount to a rather frail memorial of a fleeting time, but we took them out, one by one, dusted them off, and scanned them. Sheelagh spread a blanket on the kitchen floor, and we poured out the coins, the children running their fingers like misers through the mound of huge pennies, at last convinced that we had put in the day to some point. There were three small plastic biplanes that Jasper had reluctantly sacrificed from his toy hoard at the time; there was a photograph of Jeff, Borges, and Jasper taken at the front door of Pilmour, Borges talking, Jeff bending to listen, a miniature Jasper mugging at the camera; there was a postcard of the Old Course with an arrow pointing out Pilmour Cottage, a piece of white quartz, a leather pouch of Jeff's that had not stood the test of time as well as the rest of the contents, a copy of the St Andrews *Citizen* dated Saturday, May 22, 1971, which we later read aloud. It might have been the current issue: the same civic preoccupations, the same cluster of local detail. There was a pen, which still wrote; there was an envelope from the Chilean Embassy in Paris addressed to me at Pilmour Cottage in Neruda's familiar green handwriting, a history examination paper of Jeff's, a copy of the St Andrews *Newsflash* — a small newspaper that Jasper and two of his schoolmates put out, and that ran for, I think, three issues.

There were separate photographs, too, of the three of us, taken roughly at that time. As we passed them round, I grew keenly aware of how differently we must be thinking, Jasper, Jeff, and I, about the piece of time that had passed between our impulsive shovelling of nine years ago and our laborious digging up of that day. For Jasper, it had been transformation — from oven height, happy and puzzled, in the way of children, to full height, a vote, and an independent being. Jeff had gone through the long tunnel of a PhD, and had probably changed least, in that he had an early serenity and his curiosity continued as alive as ever. Friendships we formed in the sixties, around that Antioch year, have remained very firm and clear to me, perhaps because, in that vivid time, the talk we had seemed always drastic, it gave off the same exhilaration that the war years did to the British, it became a defining time, and Jeff and Nora kept that directness alive: they foraged for wild plants, they read aloud to each other over the dishes, they took in the world crisply and intelligently, they thought of us exactly as we thought of them — as eternal players in a game of our own devising, fastened together by the habit of making every meeting into a celebration of that very happening, that moment. And my nine years? I had written a number of things, gone through the swirling glooms of translating, but what I think was most important to me was that after vacillating for so many years across the Atlantic, a transatlantic creature, I had shifted and had anchored myself in the Western Hemisphere. New York City is a good place to be when one has not quite decided just where to live — although I think that I have chosen looking for such a place over finding it. Apart from that, I had, as usual, changed every day.

So much for the contents of the capsule — not exactly a thrilling anthology of an epoch. But the fact that these inconsequential elements had lain underground — 'all that time,' Kate gasped, for it was longer than her life — certainly excited the children. In fact, at different times we all knelt round the blanket in the kitchen and fingered the coins — 'the real treasure,' as Sara said. The old pennies, some of them bearing the rubbed-down head of Edward VII or Queen Victoria in profile, seemed to animate us all. We rose on our knees, crowing from time to time. Fiona swooned over a twelve-sided threepenny bit from pre-decimal days. Sara was searching out the biggest and brightest — dinars, half crowns, and a single Swiss five-franc piece (which she pounced on like a buccaneer). I mooned over pesetas and duros with the obdurate profile of feeble Grandfather Franco, whose death we had waited for so long. I left them to their scrabbling and wandered back to the dining room. In truth, nothing looked any the worse for nine years in the earth except Jeff's pouch, which had yielded to green mould. But it was the card I picked up and fingered — the card on which we had signed our names to an impossibly distant intention, opening a long parenthesis in time that the exertions of the day had just closed.

The children were radiant with the occasion, as though for once life had lived up to their expectations. The rest of us were tired enough to fall asleep in the soup. We ate up the delicious remains of lunch, to save it from the pigs, to take in sustenance. We had all kept out a few coins, for sentimental rather than monetary reasons (although I admit to pocketing a sound American quarter, which had not aged beyond the point of negotiability). George seemed to me particularly broody — lugubrious, egg-bound, like the hens. We took a walk outside, he and I, in a night on which enough stars were out to confirm that they still existed.

'What's up?' I asked him.

We paced in the dark, ignoring the goats, the pigs, the chickens, the geese, the hilarity from the kitchen.

'The truth is . . .' I braced myself, for George, when he talks, is nothing if not blunt, emphatic. 'The truth is, I thought at the beginning that today was just one of your wild inventions, that kind of playing with realities you quite often do. But, I have to tell you, it has affected me a lot. I went off and sat on a log and had a long think. I even wept at one moment. I began to think about Sheelagh, about the girls, about Seggie. I tell you, my life flashed before me, probably even more than yours did.'

I was surprised, but not. George had looked all day like the practical digger, but I had seen that something was going on in the recesses of his being.

'I've decided something,' he said. 'And I don't think I'll tell the others until tomorrow. But that box of yours moved me a lot. I looked at Rona, the dog, and thought, Well, she certainly won't be here ten years from now. Then I looked at Sheelagh, myself, the children, Seggie, you, everything — heavens, it all seemed so frail and vulnerable that I decided, Tomorrow we're going to bury a capsule of our own. Ten years from now, Janie will be eighteen, Sheelagh and I will be forty, we move at such a rate that we're bound to be somewhere else — I don't mean physically, I mean in how we see things. So I'm going to tell them all tomorrow at breakfast to get things ready for a capsule, and we'll bury it just before sunset. Ten years seems a good time. Sheelagh and I have a twentieth wedding anniversary then, and I know we'll still be married, still misfiring but married, and I just don't want this sense of continuing time to end, I just want there to be another knot waiting in the string for all of us.'

I felt warmly toward George at that moment, but even so, I had had my share of time capsules for one day. I suggested we put in things from our capsule. Apart from the card (and what remained of Jeff's leather pouch), everything in it might as well go on in time, as far as I was concerned.

We went in. The children had claimed Allen as a private possession, and he rose to their demands. Allen had surprised us all, arriving as the only stranger at the feast and yet entering in with exuberance and good humour. He patiently pointed out Hawaii to them in the atlas and taught them to pronounce it correctly; he was for them too good to be true, better than *Dallas* (a rerun of which Jane had missed, unperturbed). He became their hero, far more fascinating to them than any of the rest of us — their parents, especially. 'Wee Allen', they called him, to their own squeaky delight. We all had our fair share of blisters and aches, and I went off to bed. Jasper came in at some point and sat on the end of my bed, and we talked, drowsily, about the amazement of the day, of arriving after such shifting, such wandering. It was a point of arrival we would remember, a good moment to go to sleep on.

We all turned up in the kitchen the next morning in a fairly desultory order — at least until George came in and told the children what he had in mind. Immediately, they were seized with a kind of capsule fever and went off in all directions to gather treasures worthy of the occasion, piling them in the dining room. Summer had come out for the day — a warm, hazy heat, an enveloping greenness. Jasper looked quite dazed, grinning and shaking his head. Sheelagh shot off somewhere in the car. We interviewed the children with a small tape recorder, asking them what they thought they would be doing ten years from now. Kate said she wanted a baby. Sara, tired of being small, said she wanted to be as tall as Allen. We all added our own adages. George, who had not been about all morning, turned up with a fat sealed envelope and a brooding expression. I cannot imagine what he had written — but then perhaps I can.

The details of the day are blurred; about six, we gathered in the dining room again, and, through a rather painful process of elimination (it had to be made clear to Sara that if she buried her favourite small blanket she would, of course, not have it around), we eventually filled three vast plastic boxes, wrote out the appropriate documents, signed them, sealed everything up. The experience of the previous day had left its mark: we wrapped the boxes in aluminium foil for the metal detectors of the future, and picked out a spot equidistant from three trees — a holly, a chestnut, and a sycamore. George dug a deep, immaculate hole, and we all trooped out, planted the gleaming boxes in the bottom, took stock for a moment, and then shovelled back the dirt, taking turns to tamp the surface level. As the sun was going down, we lit a bonfire over in the grove where the goats lived, and sat about on tree stumps drinking hot chocolate, gazing into the fire, while the goats nuzzled our knees and nibbled at our shoelaces. One by one, the children began to droop and were carried off to bed. Jane looked rapt. I asked her what she was thinking about. 'Nothing very much', she said. 'But I like best of all being here listening to what people say.' The fire began to die, and the dark came down.

*

That's just about it. Such a small event, and yet the ripples from it ran across the pools of our attention, stopped us, affected us. The next day, Jeff, Nora, Allen, Jasper, and I, after returning the metal detector to a delighted Mrs Brian, took off for a five-day drive through the places of my past — to the Border country, drizzling and dotted with sheep, past the gloomy depths of St Mary's Loch, all the way to gentle Galloway, grass-green, smelling of warm damp, to that village of milk and honey, to the house I was born in — stopping to see friends on the way. We told the story of the box in the ground once, maybe twice, and then we stopped, because it was complete in our minds and it was actually quite complicated to tell, as I have discovered. I have found that the telling resembles picking at a loose thread in a piece of whole cloth — seemingly simple to disentangle but winding in eventually a great intricacy of warp and woof, threads that lead in unimagined directions. I did not realize that in digging up that fairly inconsequential box, that whim of ours, I would be digging up a great deal more. Significantly, while we were digging that day away it was the roots that gave us the most trouble. But we covered them over again, and they will clearly endure. I think, in fact, that I am done with the metaphor of roots. I prefer that of a web, a web of people and places, threads of curiosity, wires of impulse, a network of the people who have cropped up in our lives, and will always crop up — 'the webbed scheme', as Borges calls it.

There are many threads I did not unravel, many things I skipped over, inevitably, because I had not intended at all to wind in the fabric of the past — a precarious dimension, I think, for even in going over essential pieces of it I realize how much we all edit what has happened to us, how much we all make acceptable, recountable versions of past events. Mulling them over, as I have had to do, I find that sometimes the version and the grainy reality become separated: not contradictory but separated.

I have not spoken of many things. I have not

mentioned money, for example. Living by writing, I had an income over the years like a fever chart, but there was always work to do, there was always translating, which I did as a kind of warm-up to the day's work; there was always enough to keep us going. If we needed money, I worked hard; if not, I idled. I have not mentioned various women, who moved in and out of our lives, who were woven into our existence, shifting, affecting. I have not mentioned solitude, which was an inevitable accompaniment to those years. I used to meet the English writer J.G. Ballard from time to time in London. He had raised his children by himself after the death of his wife, and he once said to me, 'Remember, if you are a single father, it's lucky you're a writer, because you can stay home all the time, you have the time for it.' He always cheered me up. Nor did I feel so very solitary. Jasper was the best of company. But there was an essential solitude, the *soledad* of García Márquez, or of Melissa in Lawrence Durrell's *Mountolive*: '*Monsieur, je suis devenue la solitude même.*' And I saved, on the bulletin board we set up wherever we came to rest, a clipping from an interview that Truman Capote once gave: 'Writers just tend to learn more than other people how to be alone. They learn to be dependent on themselves . . . it just has to be that; there's no way of getting around it.' Although Jasper alleviated that essential solitude, I fear that some of it has settled on him, by unavoidable osmosis.

I say 'we' too often when I am talking about Jasper,

but I have no intention of implying any unanimity of mind. We functioned as a unit, but for me the whole business of raising children meant teaching them to fly, separately and independently, getting them ready for leaving. I have been much preoccupied by fatherhood, for I felt most close to my own quiet father, and Jasper I have known as well as I know anyone. One moment lives vividly in my remembering. We had travelled up to Scotland during our houseboat days, on a visit, and we descended from the London train in the wan light of early morning, on the platform at St Boswells, where my father was waiting. The train chuffed off, and, standing in the rising steam, there were the three of us: Jasper, small and eager, my father, pleased and open-eyed, and I, standing between them, father and son at once. That moment dissipated with the steam, and Jasper and I have exchanged the state of being father and son for that of inhabiting our separate solitudes.

And Scotland? It no longer seems a contradiction to me, nor am I inclined to rant about Calvin the way I once did. I have, besides, a stake in its future. On August 7, 1990, I have to be there, Jeff and Nora will certainly be there, Jasper will turn up from who knows where, Allen has promised his presence, Sheelagh will arrive, breathless but in time, George will have the spades ready, and Jane, turned eighteen, Kate, in a totally different shape, little sparky Sara, and Kirsty, who by then will be older than Jane is now — they will be there. Scotland has re-formed itself, in my mind, into the particularities of last summer, a time capsule in itself.

I call Sheelagh on the phone, tell her I am finishing writing the story of the summer. I have in front of me the card we all signed — Jeff, Jasper, and I — and a leaf from the elm tree that sheltered the box, already dried and cracking. A few odds and ends of the story are still lying about, untold. I ask her about the children, the goats, the household. She fires all the news to me.

'When are you coming back?' she asks me suddenly.

'One of these days,' I say to her. I might have added, 'If we're spared.' I do now, but in the nuclear, not the Calvinist sense.

*

The evening I finished writing all this down, at the remove of New York City, resisting the temptation to pick at still another thread, and ready to leave Scotland alone, at least until 1990, I stopped off on the way home for a drink with two old friends, Linda and Aaron Asher.

'What have you been up to?' Aaron asked me, in a misguided moment.

I told him, in the briefest, most encapsulated form.

'But didn't you see today's *Times*?' he said, going to fetch it and ripping out the relevant page.

Here is the story in its entirety, page B2, April 24 issue:

It may be the ultimate skyscraper both aesthetically and because of its superb construction, but the Empire State Building has not completely withstood the ravages of time.

A time capsule placed in the building's cornerstone on Sept. 9, 1930, by Alfred E. Smith, then former Governor, was removed yesterday in preparation for the building's 50th anniversary celebration next week. The copper box that contained the time capsule was full of water, and most of the contents had been destroyed.

The seams of the box, which evidently had not been properly sealed, had split, according to a spokesman for the building. The pre-cast concrete slab under which the box had rested had not been cemented into place. As a result, all the papers, which included a copy of the *New York Times* of Sept. 9, 1930, pictures relating to the building and paper currency from $1 up to $100 — had disintegrated.

In Scotland, enduring is a much graver matter.

Afterword

When I finished writing the story of digging up Scotland, I felt as if some ancient, dark creature had risen from my shoulders and flapped its ungainly way across the horizon. The flow of time, however, did not stop.

On December 20, 1983, Rona, the McQuittys' dog, died.

On May 14, 1984, Sheelagh McQuitty died, after struggling valiantly against an indefatigable cancer.

On June 9, 1985, Charlie Drummond died, cheerful, in mid-sentence.

On August 7, 1990, we did regather in Fife, with even more attendant children. We found the capsules easily this time; but there were shadows across the morning. It was the children who lit up immediately at the idea of another capsule, an agestone in their unmarked future, and they set about preparing it. I chose neither to contribute to it nor to attend its burial. By now, I felt, I needed no extra evidence of the ways in which time passes.

Recently, I received a clipping from *The St Andrews Citizen* of April 18, 1997, sent to me by a kindly librarian in St Andrews, stony death-notice in the form of the Links Council to demolish Pilmour Cottage. It will continue to exist, however, in the form of a fiction, as do our dear dead.

Waiting for Columbus

For some time, I viewed the coming of 1992 with a certain dread. It could hardly have escaped anyone's attention then that on October 12 five hundred years had passed since Christopher Columbus first stepped ashore on what was for him a new world, however ancient its inhabitants. From the vantage point of Europe, he began to make a vast unknown into a known, and the date has been nailed down in history as that of the discovery of America. Not surprisingly, 1992 lay steadily in the sights of many quickening interests, public and private, and countless plans were laid to turn the year into a circus of near-global celebration. It is understandable that governments should seize on such occasions for a bit of national brio, the satisfaction of having come a long way. It puts some kind of affirmative stamp on a doubtful present; and, besides that, it gives a year a 'theme', which can be echoed inexhaustibly in exploitable form. The year 1992 was a prospective gold mine: the books, bumper issues of magazines, television specials, documentaries, simulations, and reenactments, and the coins, medallions, ship models, maps, museum exhibits, and other icons. One Spanish sculptor, Antoni Miralda, set in motion plans for a symbolic marriage between the Statue of Liberty and the statue of Columbus that stands on a cast-iron column overlooking the harbour of Barcelona. Outsized wedding garments and jewellery were put on display in various capital cities, and the symbolic ceremony was held on St Valentine's Day in Las Vegas. It occurred to me that if only Columbus had had the foresight to acquire the fifteenth-century equivalent of an agent his descendants would have raked in much more gold than even the Admiral dreamed of amassing, abundant though these dreams were, during his various sallies westward.

Of the thirty-odd countries that pledged themselves to official quincentenary fervour, Spain outdid all the others in extravagance, spending hundreds of millions of dollars on the event. Spain, after all, made the initial investment in the Admiral's enterprise, and clearly looked to 1992 as a way of reaping even more than it already had from that first outlay. That year, Spain was the setting for a World's Fair (in Seville) and for the Olympic Games (in Barcelona), and Madrid was named Europe's City of Culture for the year. All these events attracted intrusions of tourists — tourism being an industry that Spain has been turning to great advantage since the sixties. Spain was ripe for a year of self-congratulation: since the death of Francisco Franco, in 1975, it has made itself into a responsible and sophisticated modern democracy, an active and energetic member of the European Community, with a new and zippy life style and an aggressive self-confidence. Spain trumpeted the quincentenary: in 1988, the Spanish government established a foundation in Washington, DC — SPAIN '92 — 'to engage Americans in a thoughtful exploration of the impact of Christopher Columbus's voyages and to strengthen the cultural traditions which unite Americans and Spaniards', in the words of its brochure. Spain also had built meticulous replicas of the three ships that made the first voyage — the Santa Maria, of a design the Spanish called a *nao*, slower and statelier than the caravels Niña and Pinta. They were launched by members of the Spanish Royal Family in the fall of 1989, and set sail in a reenactment of the voyage. Later they showed themselves around the Caribbean before turning up to lead the tall ships into New York Harbour on the Fourth of July. They were not, however, the only replicas of that little fleet; several were built — enough to stage a round-the-world caravel race if they all remained afloat after their strenuous year of simulation. One replica of the Santa Maria was built in Barcelona by a Japanese publisher, who intended to sail it all the way from Barcelona to Kobe, Japan, thus fulfilling Columbus's original plan, which was to find the trade route from Spain to the lucrative East.

Ever since the quincentenary loomed, however, there arose a countercry, close to an outcry, over the global fiesta, and it mostly came, understandably, from the countries of Spanish America — the discoverees, as it were, which were of course given no choice about being discovered. What came to these countries with the conquest was nothing good — violent invasion, massacre, enslavement, exploitation — and a number of voices strongly suggested that 1992 be observed as a year of mourning in Spanish America and the Caribbean. Cuba was scathing in its denunciations of the celebrations. I was sent a copy of the *Declaration of Mexico*, circulated by a group for the 'Emanicipation and Identity of Latin America'. To give the declaration's gist, I quote its first and last articles:

> Whereas October 12, 1492, which according to a Eurocentric version of history was the 'discovery' and/or 'encounter between two worlds', marked the beginning of one of the greatest acts of genocide, pillage, and plunder in human history, and whereas the intention to celebrate its 500th Anniversary constitutes an act of arrogance and disdain for the peoples of the Third World . . .
> . . . we have resolved not to participate in any activity related to the official celebrations of the 500th Anniversary, since such participation would legitimize the historical system of injustice and dependence initiated on October 12, 1492, and the spurious character of its celebration.

Rumblings from Latin America notwithstanding, the country that dressed the quincentenary in the most

official pomp and gravity was the Dominican Republic, which, with Haiti, occupies the island Columbus
christened Hispaniola — the first whole territory subdued and settled by the fortune hunters from Spain.
Santo Domingo, the present-day capital, was the first
outpost, the first colonial city in the New World, and
its cathedral contains at least some of the Admiral's
remains. (Havana and Seville claim to have the other
parts in their keeping.) For the country's President, Dr
Joaquin Balaguer, then eighty-four, the quincentenary
had been an obsession from an early age, and his long
life seemed to have been single-mindedly aimed at
October 12, 1992. As far back as 1986, Balaguer instituted the Permanent Dominican Commission for the
Fifth Centenary of the Discovery and Evangelization
of America — the longest and most pompous banner
flown in the name of the event. He appointed as head
of the commission his close friend and ecclesiastical
henchman the Archbishop of Santo Domingo, Nicolás
López Rodríguez, who viewed the landing of Columbus
as the most momentous event in Christendom since the
Resurrection. Balaguer clearly expected the quincentenary to bring to his country an attention and a sense
of importance until now earned only by a rich crop of
exceptional baseball players. Columbus, in his *Journal
of the First Voyage*, speaks of the island as 'the fairest
ever looked on by human eyes' — an endorsement
that is still used liberally by the Dominican Tourist Office.

The country certainly seemed so to me when I first

went there, over ten years ago. Outside its capital and two or three lesser cities, it is rural and agricultural, dotted sparsely with small villages, outposts of subsistence, so that its beautiful and immensely varying landscapes always dominate. Dominicans are among the most cheerful people in the world, and I found myself going back to explore further. I eventually settled on the Samaná Peninsula, in the extreme northeast of the country, a narrow arm of land, thirty-two miles in length, that protrudes from the bulk of the mainland like a lobster claw into the Atlantic and forms a very long and narrow bay on its south side — a natural harbour that at different times has attracted the acquisitive attention of foreign powers, the United States among them. A low mountain spine runs along the peninsula, falling away on the north to a long sand coast and on the south to strings of beaches and small enclosed inlets. The whole peninsula is covered with coconut palms, whose easygoing crop has been for many years its principal source of revenue. Samaná is quite literally the end of the line: if you follow its single road to the tip of the peninsula, you find yourself facing a white beach, a reef, and beyond, the open Atlantic. It was on Samaná that Columbus made his last landfall on the first voyage of discovery, and from there he set sail for Spain with news of what he had found.

As a place, Samaná is one of those geographical oddities which seem to invite a correspondingly eccentric history: it feels itself only marginally connected to the rest of the country; on early maps, it is sometimes shown as an island. A broad expanse of marsh — the estuary of the River Yuna, which flows into Samaná Bay — joins it to the mainland. In the past, most likely, the marsh did provide a shallow waterway across the neck of the peninsula to the north coast, an escape route for privateers bottled up in the bay when piracy was at its height on the Spanish Main. In those days, Samaná afforded just the kind of retreat the buccaneers needed; and, indeed, it has given refuge to a great variety of runaways in its long past. It has the look and feel of an island, and it has an islandlike history — a series of intrusions and violations, all coming from the outside. It is one of the poorest provinces in the country, with the leanest statistics, but the land is bountiful, and its inhabitants follow a way of life that has allowed them to survive, however frugally, for an immemorial time.

In the sixteenth and seventeenth centuries, Samaná was often raided by English and Spanish ships in search of buccaneers and runaways. It was not until 1756 that a group of Spanish colonists was shipped from the Canary Islands to found the town of Santa Barbara de Samaná. In 1807, while the French were briefly in possession of the entire island, General Louis Ferrand, Napoleon's commander in Santo Domingo, published a detailed plan for a new port, with a miniature French city neatly squared beside it, to be built in Samaná and named Port Napoleon: Samaná was to become a rich coffee plantation, Port Napoleon 'a cultural capital between East and West'. General Ferrand died, and the French lost possession of the island before the work was begun, but the plans for Port Napoleon still exist. Between 1850 and 1874, the United States Congress was seriously studying a plan first to rent and then to annex the Samaná Peninsula, and establish a permanent naval station in Samaná Bay. The idea of acquiring Samaná for the United States was something of a fixation in the mind of William H. Seward, who was Secretary of State under Presidents Lincoln and Johnson, and who had previously engineered the purchase of Alaska from the Russians. On three or four occasions, agreement seemed close, but Congress voted against annexation, and when further offers to lease Samaná Bay were made General Ignacio María González, newly elected President in Santo Domingo, took a firm and popular decision that no part of his country should be yielded up to foreign ownership. The Germans and the English had also shown a commercial interest in Samaná. Even so, the place was hardly prosperous: the population of the peninsula when annexation was being considered was under three thousand.

Samaná had received an intrusion of settlers in 1824, when President Jean-Pierre Boyer of Haiti, who had just occupied Santo Domingo, decided to ship in immigrants from the southern United States to populate the remoter parts of his new colony. Some three hundred of them settled in Samaná, and you can still hear the sing-song English of their descendants in the market, or shake the huge hand of a man named Samuel Johnson on the dock. Don León, who keeps our local store, tells me of his childhood in Samaná, some sixty years ago, when there was no road to town and he had to row to market — a two-hour haul — sometimes twice a day. But he remembers a Samaná that was more prosperous than now, with a chocolate factory, an icehouse, a soap works, and a busy maritime trade. Samaná harbour is now mostly a landfall for small boats making an Atlantic crossing or cruising the Caribbean. In January, when the trade winds are blowing right, we see them straggle in, flying a variety of flags, sea-weary. Last winter, I found a plastic pouch of water on the beach with instructions in Norwegian. I do not know Norwegian, so I added its contents to the sea.

It was Samaná itself, and not Columbus, that drew me in. Turns in the road revealed sudden beauties, to gasp at. Everything moved at walking pace. A car looked somehow absurd there. The place felt as if it were adrift, unanchored to anything. I explored the villages and the coast, I asked questions, I listened a lot, and eventually I acquired a piece of land just inside the point where Samaná Bay opens to the Atlantic: land that rose in a broad bowl from a small enclosed beach to a ridge, and fell away to the road on the other side; land that faced south across the bay and was thickly overgrown — well staked with coconut palms, all nodding seaward. Don Justo, who sold me the land, told me that he had not seen it in years, although he lives only a few miles from it. He had sent a man four times a year to gather the coconuts, but he did not think much else could grow there. Now he comes often, amazed that I have coaxed it into fruit.

In the Dominican countryside, campesinos live mostly in clumps of houses, settlements rather than villages — *aldea* is the Spanish word — that are dotted here and there, usually close to a water source. My land fell away steeply on the west side to a small, flat clearing through which a freshwater stream flowed by way of a small lagoon into the sea. Five houses stood close to the stream, accommodating in all about twenty people — men, women, a tribe of children. After buying the land, I made arrangements to stay in a room in one of the houses, and I hired the men of the *aldea* to help me build a small house, and to clear the land for cultivation. During that time, I got to know my neighbours very well indeed. We were some nine miles beyond the last town — that is, beyond public market, post office, electricity, telephone, hospital, and hardware store — and everybody depended on the small country *colmados*, which sold the basics: rice, oil, sugar, salt, rum. What we lived in — our bounded world — was, I learned from them, our *vecindad*, or neighbourhood, which meant roughly the piece of coast you could encompass with a sweep of the arm from the ridge. Within the *vecindad,* you knew the inhabitants, down to the babies, and if you did not actually know them you had heard about them, in story form, and you inevitably shared their crises and daily dramas.

When you settle in a place, what you absorb, and to some extent take on, from those who live there is their vantage point: the way they see the rest of the world, their preoccupations, the web of their attention. Most of my neighbours are *analfabetos;* they neither read nor write. They are, however, passionate, dedicated talkers, often eloquent. Their mode, their natural wavelength, is to put themselves in story form. Their lives have no written archives, their years no numbers or dates; for that reason, a quincentenary is meaningless to them. They have saved their personal history in the form of a set of stories, well polished with telling, stored, ready. I have heard some of them recount their lives, a rosary of stories, on different occasions, and noticed how they vary with the telling. Everything that happens eventually circulates in story form, embellished by its tellers. Don León listens avidly to the radio news in his store and passes on his edited versions of it to his customers, who disperse it further on the way home. Travelling so, from teller to teller, quite ordinary happenings often turn into wonders.

In 1950, George F. Kennan made an investigatory journey through a number of Latin American countries. On his return, he wrote a report that was not circulated at the time, but that he refers to in his memoirs. I quote one passage:

> The price of diplomatic popularity, and to some extent of diplomatic success, is constant connivance at the maintenance of a staggering and ubiquitous fiction: the fiction of extraordinary human achievement, personal and collective, subjective and objective, in a society where the realities are almost precisely the opposite, and where the reasons behind these realities are too grim to be steadily entertained. Latin American society lives, by and large, by a species of make-believe: not the systematized, purposeful make-believe of Russian communism, but a highly personalized, anarchical make-believe, in which each individual spins around him, like a cocoon, his own little world of pretense, and demands its recognition by others as the condition of his participation in the social process.

I can feel the exasperation behind that passage: the exasperation of a diplomat accustomed to clarity; the same exasperation that travellers in a Western hurry will stumble over in Latin America. Yet Kennan is putting his finger on a linguistic mode that is familiar to anyone who has lived in the countries of Spanish America, that I come across every day in conversations with my neighbours, that is at the core of Borges's writings. To Borges, everything put into language is a fiction, and should not be confused with reality. The fictions we make are ways of ordering and dominating the disorders of reality, even though they in no way change it. The 'truth' of a fiction is less important than its effectiveness; and, since reality is shifting and changing, our fictions must constantly be revised. For my neighbours, their stories are a form of continuous self-creation, and a way of taming and domesticating the world outside the *vecindad*, the great, fearful unknown.

This fictive cast of mind, while it animates the *chisme* — the daily gossip that serves as our newspaper — is something of an impediment to serious discourse. I sometimes notice in the discussion I listen to on Dominican radio that what takes place is less an exchange of views on a given question than a series of restatements of the question, each distinctly personal, each with a neat resolution. It is perhaps too extreme to say of Dominicans that they are devoid of objectivity, yet that is what I often feel. It is as though they had no overall grasp of their own situation, even though they have at the ready a rich variety of explanations and personal remedies. For them, once a problem has been put right in words, it can be forgotten. The reality is another matter altogether.

Listening to the Spanish spoken in the Dominican Republic, I quite often come on words so bizarrely unfamiliar that I have to reach their meaning by scrutinous questioning, for I have never heard them anywhere else. One such word, of Afro-Hispanic origin, from the language arrived at by the Africans brought as slaves to Hispaniola, is the noun *fucú* or *fukú*. It is often spoken with a certain dropping of the voice. *Un fucú* is something ill-omened, likely to bring bad luck, something in a person or a place or a happening that has doom about it. At the materialization of a *fucú* in any form, Dominicans cross their index fingers in the air and exclaim '*Zafa!*' — loosely translated as 'Change the subject.' At least they used to, I am told by the elders in my neighbourhood: perhaps the custom has waned because there are so many obvious public *fucús* in the country now that the day would be one long '*Zafa!*' The word has entered not just my vocabulary but my consciousness; I am able to realize that some people and elements in New York have a *fucú* about them for me. It helps me save time.

The most interesting *fucú* of all among Dominicans, however, is the superstition that has existed for centuries that bad luck would dog anyone who spoke aloud the name of Cristóbal Colón. That called for instant crossed fingers and a loud '*Zafa!*' One referred instead to the Admiral, or the Discoverer. The official propaganda surrounding the quincentenary has had to face down the *fucú*, as it were, for the name has somehow kept coming up. But the campesinos still believe in the *fucú* that C—— C—— brings bad luck, perhaps with more fervour now than before. One of my neighbours told me solemnly that the word *colonia* — 'colony' — came from the name of Cristóbal Colón, an error I saw no point in correcting.

In the evenings of those first days, when we had finished work and bathed and eaten, we would sit by the stream and talk as the dark came down. My neighbours were full of questions, mostly about life in the United States, which I answered with some care; and in my turn I questioned them closely about their lives and the ways of the place. We have continued so ever since. In the evenings I hear feet on the stones of my terrace, and someone will materialize, always with an offering — Sandro with fish, Felipe with an egg — and we will sit on the warm stone and talk. A kind of natural barter plays a large part in my neighbours' existence, and, indeed, they like nothing better than a 'deal', an exchange that pleases both sides. I have to remember that I am a *patrón*, a landowner, and I have to assume the role sometimes: to settle a dispute, or to come up with money for medicine — a debt that is always paid off with a day's work. Dominican society is a curious web of family connections, of debts and favours owed, of patronage and reward — a system that, while it functions well enough in remote country settlements like ours, has turned Dominican politics into a tangle of corruption. My neigbours are natural anarchists. Pucho, who has worked with me since the beginning, and now lives, with his family, on the land above mine, insists that he has no loyalties other than to what his eye encompasses, and he leaves no ground unplanted, for that is what makes unquestionable sense to him. One evening, he found, in a catalogue that had come with my mail, a rowing machine. He was delighted, for he has a long row to the reef where he goes fishing, and hates rowing; when I explained that people in cities had rowing machines in their houses to keep healthy, he looked at me pityingly.

As I discovered by the stream, history for my neighbours is mostly hearsay, vague rumblings in a dateless clutter of past, anchored by a few facts brought home from school by the children. For most of them, the past, though it has engendered their present, is an irrelevance. So at one point, for a few evenings running, I told them a fairly simplified version, though quite a detailed one, of Cristóbal Colón and the first voyage, the first landings, the coming of the Spaniards, and the subsequent enslavement of their country. I told them what I knew about the Indians — the Tainos and the Ciguayos — who when Colón arrived had been living an unvarying rural existence. They made their settlements by fresh water, close to the sea. They fished, they bartered work and harvests, they lived communally. They were also innocent of money, as my neighbours often are, though not from choice.

Some of my neighbours became quite indignant at my version of the arrival of the Spaniards, and, indeed, I did myself. Although I had read fairly extensively about the conquest, I had always done so in the historical mass, so to speak; I had never been physically close to the scene before, and I felt myself suddenly waking up to those happenings as quite easily imaginable realities. When the house was finished and the books were unpacked, I started to read that history all over again, beginning with where I was — with Columbus's landing on Samaná — and then going mostly backward, reading what I could find about the conditions of life in Hispaniola before that catastrophic disembarkation.

*

In early January of 1493, aboard the Niña, with the Pinta in attendance, Columbus was bowling along the north coast of Hispaniola, on an easterly course. Of all his landfalls so far, Hispaniola had proved the most rewarding. Its natives were friendly and docile, its vegetation was sumptuous, and he had found enough gold to fuel expectations of more. It would be his territory, he had decided, his base for any future exploration. Fixed firmly in his sailing mind, however, was the urge to return to Spain with all dispatch, on the first good wind. He had lost the Santa María, grounded on a coral reef on Christmas Eve, but its timbers had been used to build a small fort called La Navidad, where the Admiral left behind a garrison of thirty-nine men. The standard histories have him rounding the northeast corner of the Samaná Peninsula and deciding to make one last landfall, to take on fresh water and provisions for the return crossing, and, if possible, to careen and caulk his two remaining boats, which were taking water. According to his log entry for January 12, 1493, the two ships entered 'an enormous bay three leagues wide, with a little island [*una isleta pequeñuela*] in the middle of it', and they anchored between the little island and a shallow sand beach. The following morning, the Admiral sent a boat ashore to treat with the Indians, as he had been doing with regularity over the past three months. These Indians, however, were quite different in appearance from the ones so far encountered. These wore their hair long, plaited with bird plumage, and they blackened their faces. Also, unlike most of those so far encountered, they carried arms — longbows and arrows. The crew persuaded one of them to return to the ship and talk with the Admiral. By this time, the Spaniards had most likely acquired a certain basic vocabulary, and, as usual, the Admiral questioned the man assiduously on the whereabouts of gold, and delivered an invitation to his cacique, his chief. The Indian was fed, given some trinkets, and returned by the boat's crew to his beach. On this occasion, some fifty-five Indians had gathered, and seven of the boat's crew bargained for bows and arrows, as they had been ordered. They had acquired two bows when something caused the Indians to go back to collect their arms. Leaving nothing to chance, the seven Spaniards attacked them, wounding one Indian with a sword slash in the buttocks and another in the breast with a crossbow arrow. This brief skirmish, most likely founded on a misunderstanding, has gone into the annals as the first shedding of indigenous blood in the New World — the first, faint inkling of the slaughter that was to follow. Three days later, the wind turned westerly, and, with four of the long-haired Indians added to the onboard evidence of the New World, the Niña and the Pinta put out well before dawn and set course for Spain. In his log the Admiral referred to his last anchorage as the Golfo de las Flechas, the Bay of the Arrows.

The Journal of the First Voyage, the written source of the discovery, is a strangely diffuse document, very far from objectivity even when it is being a ship's log, for some of its landfalls are still being argued over. (There is no original of the document. The version we read is an annotated text of a 1530s edition prepared and in many instances paraphrased by a later visitor, the diligent friar Bartolomé de Las Casas, from a less than complete copy made by an errant scribe; but not even this text was known about until 1825, when it was published, circulated, studied, and, in 1828, translated into English.) Some of the journal is first person, some third person (Las Casas's paraphrase), some in the shorthand of terse nautical observation. Columbus's own observations sometimes have the true awe of a man seeing unimagined wonders for the first time, but they are interspersed with passages of self-congratulation, lavish reassurances to Their Majesties, small sermons and other bursts of missionary zeal, inflated promises of bountiful gold, and a very eccentric geography. Columbus was in his forties by then, and for the last ten years his sole preoccupation had been to persuade some rich and powerful patron to underwrite an expedition of discovery. He had presented his arguments many times — as often as possible — first to the Portuguese court and then to Their Catholic Majesties in Spain, and he had obviously made them as alluring as he could. He was familiar with Marco Polo's chronicles, and cast his own expectations in the same high tone, conjuring up a vision of a New World that, since it was so far entirely imagined, could be wondrous in every respect. He became a practised exaggerater. He was shrewd enough to realize that he had to satisfy a multitude of interests, and his arguments were consequently many-faceted: for mercantile interests he would discover the route to the East that would open up trade with Cathay and with Cipango (Japan); for the Crown he would claim all new lands and found for Spain a colonial empire; for the Church he could promise converts, he would find the Garden of Eden; and beyond all these interests he dangled the promise of gold in abundance, at a time when Spain's treasury was exhausted. He had voiced these expectations so often that when he did find land what he looked for first was a self-justifying confirmation of them. His New World existed for him in the fiction he had made of it before he discovered it, and there was often a considerable disparity between what he found and what he said he found. After exploring the coast of Cuba, in November, he insisted, and continued to insist, that it was Cathay; yet he did not continue west. By then, from the natives he encountered he had picked up enough stories of gold for it to be fixed abidingly in the forefront of his attention. For him, the rumour of gold brought wish and reality together. Forgetting about the East, he followed the Indians' indications and turned back in the direction of Hispaniola.

Among a handful of anecdotes that Dominicans like to tell about the conquest is one that I have heard in a few variant forms. As fact it is improbable, but as essence it is peerless. It became the practice of the caciques to retreat from the arriving Spaniards, leaving placatory gifts in their path. The story has one such cacique leaving as an offering his beautiful daughter, bound to a stake, and wearing nothing but a gold ring in her nose. The Admiral, arriving at the head of his men, stops them suddenly with spread hands, gazes at the girl for a gravid minute, then points a trembling finger and asks, 'Where did you get that ring?'

I keep thinking of those first encounters, particularly from the point of view of language. The Spaniards and the Indians had no language in common, and Columbus had to communicate as tourists do nowadays in markets beyond their linguistic reach — by pointing and gesticulating. While that probably served well enough to get the ships' companies food and water, to make gestures of friendship and good intentions, and even to emphasize a particularly urgent interest in anything made of gold, it cannot have made possible the communication of anything abstract, like the claiming of all the Indians' lands in the name of Ferdinand and Isabella, or the fundamental tenets of the Holy Roman Church. Over various landfalls, the Spaniards probably began to assemble a sketchy vocabulary of native words, but there are signs in the journal that Columbus was prone to the affliction of beginners in any language — an overwillingness to understand. Hearsay for Columbus was whatever he thought he heard, and hearsay was the basis of his golden promises in a famous letter that he addressed to Their Majesties on the return crossing. Besides the gold and the Indians, Columbus was carrying back with him a great fund of information that he had sifted from the Indians' stories, some of it more imagined than real. *The Journal of the First Voyage* has a kind of speculative edge to it, an awe in its voice, a looking-at that before very long became a looking-for. The second voyage, from 1493 to 1496, was no longer looking for gold; it was going after it. With the second voyage, the conquest really began.

On the first voyage, Columbus went through an orgy of naming — christening capes, headlands, bays, points, rivers, and islands, and entering the names meticulously in his log. For him, giving them Spanish names was synonymous with claiming them for Spain, and his naming grew more diligent as the voyage progressed. No matter that everything was already named and understood by the Indians — from now on, Spain was to impose itself on Hispaniola, a God-appointed enterprise. Whatever form of life the Indians had achieved up until now was an irrelevance, since it was about to be ended, irrevocably.

The landfall in Columbus's Bay of the Arrows, of first-blood fame, is identified in the vast majority of books about Columbus as the beach called Las Flechas, on the south coast of the Samaná Peninsula. Facing that beach is a small, neat jewel of an island known as Cayo Levantado, assumed to be the 'little island' Columbus identifies in his log. Las Flechas lies along the coast from our beach, about a mile farther into the bay, and I must have passed it hundreds of times by now, for the road to town runs just above it. It has served to keep Columbus on my mind. The first time I explored it, I looked for some kind of marker, since Columbus's landfalls have been well labelled, but it was as anonymous as when he found it. Beyond a broad, untidy straggle of coconut palms, which always cast for me a kind of cathedral gloom on the beaches below them, lay its curve of sand, three small fishing boats pulled up, a litter of fishing gear, and Cayo Levantado riding at anchor about a mile offshore. I talked to an old man who was resting his back against one of the boats. I asked him about the beach and Columbus. 'Colón? Colón? Now, I've heard that name.'

Since about the first century, Arawak Indians had been migrating north from the South American continent through the islands, and so had settled Hispaniola a good many centuries before Columbus arrived. Those island Arawaks of Hispaniola are now generally referred to as Tainos, from the name for their upper class, for, although they had originally brought with them their own plants and methods of cultivation, they evolved a way of life distinct to the island. What we know of their mode of existence in Hispaniola has reached us mainly through the assiduousness of four chroniclers who came on subsequent voyages — Bartolomé de Las Casas, Peter Martyr, Guillermo Coma, and Gonzalo Fernández de Oviedo. Yet the more I read in the chronicles about how the Tainos lived, the more I realize that their life resembled, in most of its fundamentals, the present life of our *vecindad*. Taino artifacts are everywhere — the neighbours will bring me pieces of red pottery they come across, or an axe head, still lime-encrusted. Their life-sustaining crop was the root cassava — manioc, yucca, tapioca. It gave them bread, and they grew it in conelike mounds of earth called *conucos*. Cassava, yams, and sweet potato, along with beans, maize, peppers, and squashes, were their standard plantings, none of them at all demanding of attention or labour. They also grew cotton and tobacco and some fruit — pineapple and papaya in particular. With an abundance of fish, they were self-sufficient. A docile people, they were feudally organized under a cacique. They lived in small settlements close to fresh water, in simple houses, well roofed against the rains. Only hurricanes or droughts upset this equilibrium.

The selfsame crops are all flourishing in our *vecindad* at this moment. Pucho has a great spread of yucca growing just under the crest — a staple that feeds him year-round. Now we have additional staples — coconuts, bananas and plantains, rice, sugar, coffee, many more fruits — but the land and the fishing still provide practically all our food. Taino words are on our tongue every day — hammock, cassava, maize, tobacco, potato, canoe. Although the Taino population of Hispaniola was wiped out within thirty years of the discovery, it is as though the Tainos had left their mode of life embedded in the land, to be reenacted in a surprisingly similar form by the campesinos now. Rich soil, a benign climate, and plants of predictable yield guarantee basic survival, although today on a threadbare level. For the Tainos, however, it appears to have been an abundance, and their world was apparently both stable and peaceful. While the Tainos knew the whereabouts of gold, they made little use of it except for small ornaments. Sometimes, sitting on my terrace, I imagine what it must have been like for the Tainos, similarly perched, to see the caravels come into sight. Even today, when a boat of any size enters the bay we come out to gaze, as we do when a plane flies over.

In the letter Columbus wrote on the return crossing to Ferdinand and Isabella (it was addressed to Luis de Santangel, Crown Treasurer, for transmission to Their Catholic Majesties), he expanded on the nature of the Indians he had encountered, speaking of their timidity, their innocence, and the fact that they went unarmed and were both friendly to and fearful of the

Spaniards — perfect material for conversion and for service to the Crown. He did report, however, that he had heard of an island peopled by warlike Indians, Caribs, who were known to eat human flesh, and who made sorties on the outlying islands. The details he gave of them — that they wore their hair long and carried bows and arrows — appear to have come from the confrontation and flash of force at Las Flechas. When his boat's crew told him of that encounter, he wrote of himself in the journal, on January 13, 1493, 'In one way it troubled me, and in another way it did not, i.e., in that now they might be afraid of us. Without doubt, the people here are evil, and I believe they are from the Isle of Caribe, and that they eat men . . . If these people are not Caribes, they must at least be inhabitants of lands fronting them and have the same customs, not like the others on the other islands who are without arms and cowardly beyond reason.'

When the seventeen ships of the second voyage reached their destination in Hispaniola, with a company of about fifteen hundred, some domestic animals, and a variety of seeds, plants, and provisions, the long equilibrium that the Tainos had enjoyed ended. Columbus found the fort he had left destroyed, all the men dead — they had abused the Indians and had been overcome in turn. From this point on, Columbus never hesitated to show force in all his dealings with the Indians. They were to be subdued and turned to work in finding and extracting gold, before all else. The Spaniards as yet had no substantial permanent settlement, but they set out on expeditions to the interior, to track the gold. The course of subsequent events was perhaps set from the beginning by a fatal misunderstanding. On the first voyage, Columbus read from the gesticulations of the Indians he questioned that gold existed on the island in abundant quantities, and he reported that as fact. In truth, while gold did exist in the Cibao and in other alluvial placers, it was not widespread, plentiful, or easily accessible — certainly not to any degree that would satisfy the Admiral's by now burning expectations. Yet he continued to insist that it was, and drove the Indians more and more ferociously to produce it.

It did not take long to turn the feelings of the Tainos for the Spaniards from fear to hatred: they first rose against them in early 1494, and suffered fierce retribution. When a fleet of four ships left for Spain, in February of 1495, about five hundred Indian captives were aboard; nearly half of them died on the voyage. Columbus meanwhile set about crushing Indian resistance once and for all, which he did with a formidable force of men. He eventually secured the submission of most of the caciques, established a fort in the centre of the island, and then decided on the site of the new capital, Santo Domingo — at the mouth of the Ozama River, in the south. From every Indian over fourteen the Admiral demanded a tribute of a small piece of gold every three months.

The caciques begged to be released from the tribute of gold, offering instead to plant a vast stretch of land expressly for feeding the Spaniards, something to them of infinitely greater worth. But the Spaniards, fired by both greed and impatience, were unrelenting.

Failure to pay tribute resulted in increasingly brutal punishment — quite often, according to Las Casas, the cutting off of the Indians' hands — until, in 1497, orders came from Spain, in the form of Letters Patent, decreeing a *repartimiento*, a sharing out, of the colony. The plan was later modified to become one of granting the settlers *encomiendas*, tracts of land to use and cultivate, along with an Indian community to do each settler's bidding, with the understanding that the *encomendero* would in time convert his Indians to Christianity. The granting of *encomiendas*, however, was less about land than about Indians: in practice, a settler would be given a whole Indian community, under its cacique, to cultivate the land, to dig for gold, to do anything at all that the master might command. Religious instruction was not uppermost in the settlers' minds. By 1500, the enslavement of the Tainos was complete. The seven years of Columbus's governorship of Hispaniola had been chaotic for the Spaniards and disastrous for the Tainos. His authority over the Spanish settlers had frayed and eroded, and the revenues he had promised the Crown had not been realized. Orders came from Spain that he was to be replaced as governor by Francisco de Bobadilla; and when Bobadilla arrived in Santo Domingo, in August of 1500, his first act was to arrest Columbus and his two brothers, Bartholomew and Diego, and send them back to Spain in chains.

As for the Tainos, they were by now dwindling in number. Most of the detail that remains to us of that human erosion we owe to the extraordinarily observant and intelligent chronicle of Bartolomé de Las Casas. As a young man, in Seville, he had seen Columbus return in triumph from the first voyage in 1493, and his father and uncle had both preceded him to Hispaniola. He landed in Santo Domingo in 1502, and in his ten years there he was to bear witness to the steady extermination of the Tainos; in a growing state of moral outrage, he was led eventually to join the Dominican order and to dedicate his life to arguing the rights of the Indians and denouncing the brutalities of the conquest in his writings and in public debate in Spain. He often made his case in an eloquent polemic, but it is the details he patiently recorded in his history of the Indies which make his case for him now. He had a keen sense of the fatefulness of the times he was living in, and of the dangerous precedents being set. Were it not for him, we would know far less about the Tainos and their progressive destruction.

Among Las Casas's careful records we have his transcription of a sermon that the Dominican friar Antonio de Montesinos preached in Santo Domingo on the last Sunday of Advent, 1511, castigating the cruelty of the settlers and reminding them of their Christian obligations:

> Tell me, by what right or justice do you hold these Indians in such a cruel and horrible servitude? On what authority have you waged such detestable wars against these peoples, who dwelt quietly and peacefully on their own land? Wars in which you have destroyed such infinite numbers of them by homicides and slaughters never before heard of? Why do you keep them so oppressed and exhausted, without giving them enough to eat or curing them of the sicknesses they incur from the excessive labour you give them? And they die, or, rather, you kill them, in order to extract and acquire gold every day.
>
> And what care do you take that they should be instructed in religion, so that they may know their God and Creator, may be baptized, may hear Mass, and may keep Sundays and feast days? Are these not men? Do they not have rational souls? Are you not bound to love them as you love yourselves? Don't you understand this? Don't you feel this? Why are you sleeping in such a profound and lethargic slumber? Be assured that in your present state you can no more be saved than the Moors or Turks, who lack the faith of Jesus Christ and do not desire it.

Witnessing the massacre of Indians, Las Casas himself wrote, 'Who of those born in future centuries will believe this? I myself who am writing this and saw it and know most about it can hardly believe that such was possible.'

It may be that from the beginning the Tainos were doomed by the disturbance of their rural way of life. Their settlements were the known world to them; to be moved left them helpless. (The Spanish word *desalojamiento*, 'to be turned out of home', is a word my neighbours always utter with a hush of horror.) Their finely balanced agricultural rhythm was broken. The domestic animals — cattle, pigs, horses — that the Spaniards had brought thrived on the vegetation and trampled free over cultivated land. The Tainos, besides, had no resistance of any kind — to European diseases, to the hard labour they were subjected to in the mines, to the demands and brutalities of the settlers, to the conditions of slavery, in Hispaniola or in Spain — and they died in vast numbers. The bitter cassava has a poisonous juice, which is squeezed out before making bread; the ubiquitousness of cassava meant that for the Tainos an easy means of suicide was at hand, and they used it liberally. A few fled — some, without doubt, to the Samaná Peninsula. An outbreak of smallpox in 1518 further reduced them. Most latter-day writers on the landings of the Spaniards concur in the opinion that what probably afflicted the Tainos more than anything else was the microbes and viruses introduced by the Spaniards. Las Casas estimated that some three million Tainos had died between 1494 and 1508, a figure now considered to be an exaggeration; but, as to the Taino population, there can be no definitive figures, only guesses. What is definitive is the fact that by the 1530s virtually no Tainos were left except a few hundred who had fled to Cuba and possibly a few who survived their slavery in Spain. As a people, they were extinct.

The letter Columbus wrote to Santangel for Their Majesties, with its glowing version of what he had discovered, was printed in Barcelona in 1493, and almost immediately translated into Latin. It sketches the Indians' way of life in a mode that carries echoes of Eden, Arcadia, and Columbus's own earlier fantasies. It caught the European imagination at once, this vision of unclothed, unarmed innocence, and it was to flower later in the writings of Montaigne, in the noble savage of Rousseau, and in other written utopias. It also gave the newly discovered lands an aura of promise and freedom that served as a spur to the many westward migrations from Europe that followed. With conquest, however, the Spanish view of the Indians changed quickly. The shift is visible in Columbus's own writings: the docile Tainos, friendly, eager to please, later become 'cowards'; fear of the warlike Caribs takes precedence, a show of force is paramount. The native is animal, the paradise wilderness, both to be dominated and subdued. First seen as Ariel, the Indian is soon turned into Caliban: beast, slave, less than human.

The depletion of the Taino population left succeeding governors of Hispaniola with a serious lack of labour; new labour had to be found if the colony was to be of any further use to Spain. Hence, by

1518 African slaves were being brought to the island. They were stronger than the Tainos, better fitted for work in the mines and for cane cutting. Sugar had been introduced in 1515, and Hispaniola was turning from its exhausted gold-workings to agriculture. At the same time, however, Hispaniola was receding in importance to the Spanish Crown. In 1500 Alonso de Ojeda had discovered the coastline of what is now Colombia, with evidence of gold in quantity; and as news of that and of the later subjugation of Jamaica and Cuba, the excursions of Juan Ponce de León to Florida, in 1513, the further probing south by Vasco Núñez de Balboa, and Hernán Cortés's conquest of Mexico in 1519, filtered back steadily to Santo Domingo, many of the settlers determined to follow in these tracks and abandon the colony for more immediate reward. To survive, if not to prosper, Hispaniola needed a settled population. Instead, Santo Domingo was becoming little more than a way station on the Spanish Main. The first Spaniards came less to colonize than to return home wealthy. The surge was westward. When López de Velasco came to write the official geography of the Indies, in 1574, he reported a population in Hispaniola of a thousand Spaniards, half of them in Santo Domingo, and thirteen thousand African Negroes, with large tracts of the island abandoned. The present population of the Dominican Republic is two-thirds mulatto, one-third divided between white and black. No one claims Taino blood.

*

Although Columbus has been mythified by history as the discoverer, he cannot be made to bear the blame for the greed and the brutality of those who came after him — men of a less visionary disposition. What set the ruthless tenor of the conquest, however, was the extravagant expectations that Columbus had created in his quest for patronage. His eagerness to confirm these expectations shows in what he chose to see on the first voyage. His later life seethed with frustration, as though he could never forgive the lands he had discovered for not giving him what they had promised, or what he had made them promise. His obsession with fulfilling the expectation of abundant gold kept him from giving any thought to the territories he was meant to be governing, or maintaining any authority over the settlers. It was less the inhumanity of the settlers — although Las Casas has left us plenty of evidence of that — than the stupidity and mismanagement of the unfolding enterprise, coupled with the intrusion of disease, that made the Indians extinct in so short a time.

Living in Samaná off and on over these last years has without question made me Indian-minded in reading those chronicles. I find them horrifying. Whatever consequences the first voyage of Columbus may have had for the planet and for our present existence, I cannot see that the ensuing thirty years were other than a human disaster for Hispaniola, a record of cruel and pointless conquest that could have been otherwise.

Pucho asks me a lot about the Tainos — I once read him from Las Casas the descriptions of their common crops and agricultural practices, and he was as startled as I was that everything was all still growing within shouting distance, that we were more or less enacting the Tainos' agricultural patterns, using their words, living more or less as they did except for our clothes and our discontents. Even though the Tainos were his precursors rather than his ancestors, even though his language and his religion come from the Spaniards, it is with the Indians, the victims, that he identifies. When I told Pucho earlier this year that sometime in 1992 three caravels would sail into Samaná Bay, past our beach, to anchor off Las Flechas, and some actor would come ashore in a Columbus suit, he was all for gathering a few picked men from the *vecindad* and taking the actor hostage, as a gesture.

Legends require simplification, and by the time Columbus became legend and statue he had been enshrined as the discoverer, in some sense the founder, of the New World, although this did not really happen until the nineteenth century. Nor was it entirely a Eurocentric view that gave him the name of discoverer — it appealed as much to North Americans to fix on the image of the Admiral's first, frail landfall as a legendary beginning. The discoverees are glossed over; the fate of the Tainos is hardly common knowledge. Plans for the quincentenary made clear that in the case of Columbus the clarification of history was giving way to its Disneyfication. The image of Columbus that loomed largest was the heroic one — in television series, in two feature films, in the gloss of magazine re-creation, and in the gush of highly coloured simulation. A few years ago, an Italian film crew came to shoot part of a historical drama about Columbus on the north coast of Samaná. They used a group of villagers as extras, and left them somehow stranded in a time warp: they have never quite recovered from the experience, and talk of nothing else. In Samaná, we all felt like extras by the time the quincentenary had run its course.

By far the most imaginative suggestion I heard about an appropriate acknowledgment of the quincentenary was made on Dominican television by the Dominican economist and historian Bernardo Vega, just as President Balaguer was preparing to attend a summit meeting of Latin American and Iberian heads of state in Mexico. Vega urged him to advance the idea at the meeting that since the Club of Paris, an organization that keeps a supervisory eye on Third World debt, was already excusing the debts of some African countries, it should make the year 1992 memorable by wiping off the slate all the European debt accumulated by the countries of Latin America, as partial compensation for the wealth that had been extracted from that region, starting in 1492.

In the decade following Columbus's first landfall, the island of Hispaniola, for the Spaniards who descended on it, *was* the New World — its earliest incarnation. The first reports and chronicles also whetted the colonizing appetites of the other seafaring countries of Europe. As the conquistadores ventured farther and farther into the southern continent, establishing their maritime base at Cartagena, from which harbour the gold-bearing ships set out on the Spanish Main, a whole host of adventurers began to arrive on the scene, to take part in the general land grab in the Caribbean and to launch almost two centuries of piracy. In 1586, Sir Francis Drake occupied and sacked Santo Domingo. French buccaneers set up their harbours of operation on the island of Tortuga and on the north coast of Hispaniola, and on their sorties they also discovered the Samaná Peninsula, a natural hideout, well placed for raids on the gold lanes to the south. The remaining Spanish colonists could not muster sufficient strength to drive the French out. In 1697, they ceded the western part of the island altogether to France, and subsequently France peopled its new colony, Saint-Domingue, with bigger shipments of African slaves, to work in the increasingly lucrative sugar plantations. Spain's control of and interest in the colony waned considerably, and in 1795 it ceded the rest of the island to France. But, fired by news of the French Revolution, the slaves of Saint-Domingue began to rise in revolt, and, in 1804, succeeded in establishing the independent black republic of Haiti. Their revolutionary zeal and their determination to stamp out slavery led them into a series of aggressions against the rest of the island, and in 1822 a Haitian army occupied Santo Domingo and took over the whole island. It was the Haitian occupation that drove the colonists to unite in sufficient force to confront the invaders, to defeat them, and to declare, on February 27, 1844, the independent existence of the Dominican Republic.

The history of Hispaniola after Columbus — a history of factionalism, of foreign intrusions, of plot and counterplot — set a pattern that has continued into the island's turbulent present, and led to the republic's having had more than forty different governments between 1844 and 1916. It is a history that implies a deep division — a division between a few individuals with the ruthlessness to aspire to power and domination, on the one hand, and a quiescent people who have learned to survive whatever calamities break over their heads, on the other.

The Tainos were victims of the conquest, and, in a sense, those who have inhabited the farther reaches of the island have continued to be victims ever since. At no time was the colony free of foreign presence, of foreign domination, even after independence had been at least nominally achieved; and in this century it is the United States, rather than France or Spain, that now casts its long shadow over the island's affairs, to the point of direct intervention on two occasions. The United States Marines occupied the Dominican Republic from 1916 until 1924, when political chaos threatened civil war; and in 1965, on the same pretext, President Lyndon Johnson sent an occupying force to the island when street fighting in Santo Domingo threatened to spread and engulf the whole country. Between these two occupations came the long dictatorship of Rafael Leónidas Trujillo, who remained firmly in power from 1930 until 1961, ruling with such harsh authority that my neighbours still tend to lower their voices when they speak of his times.

I follow this history, and the history of Samaná in particular, with a kind of despairing fascination, for it reveals a pattern that I see persisting into the present — a kind of fatalistic acceptance. The Caudillo-Presidents of Dominican history — Pedro Santana, Buenaventura Baez, Ulises Heureaux — ruled as strongmen, like the caciques of old, and, in a way, laid the ground for Trujillo's absolute and unopposed rule over the country. They were his precursors. I quite often recount to Pucho what I have been reading, but it surprises him not at all, for he remembers the days of Trujillo, and finds none of the brutalities of Dominican history difficult to believe. Like all Dominicans who were alive at the time, he remembers exactly where he was when the rumour spread that El Chivo was dead. 'We did not dare to believe it at first, so we all went indoors and whispered,' he told me once. 'We stayed up all night, wondering. And then, the next morning, when the news was sure, we all went out, every single person in the village I lived in, and walked about and talked the whole day. Nobody thought about working. But we talked in whispers, because we were still afraid.'

Thirty years dead, Trujillo still mesmerizes Dominicans. In conversations he comes up all the time. '*Cuando Trujillo*' — 'in Trujillo's day' — I hear someone say, and a story will follow, of a horror, most likely, but always recounted with an edge of awe in the teller's voice. Any impending disaster — a gasoline shortage, a dearth of cement, a national strike — will cause Trujillo to be evoked: what my neighbours most fear is chaos and breakdown, and what he stamped on the country during his long rule was an unbreakable order, an authoritarian predictability. He lasted longer than any of the tyrants who preceded him, he amassed more power, property, and personal wealth, he made the military into a personal force for control, he dispensed patronage and punishment with such remorseless cunning as to paralyse his countrymen, and yet he still is remembered by a good many Dominicans as a stern father, who would take care of every eventuality, whose whims were law, but who would save them from chaos.

The mould in which Trujillo cast Dominican society has not been broken. In many ways, the country under Trujillo resembled the Hispaniola of colonial days: a feudal society with a governing elite and a large, docile peasantry. The two-thirds of the people who lived in rural areas accepted both their poverty and their powerlessness. Crime was punished mercilessly, as was opposition in any form. Life was predictable, and accepted with a fatalism that I still encounter every day. '*Somos infelices*', the rural Dominicans say very often, meaning 'It is our destiny to be poor.' At the other extreme lies the capital — Ciudad Trujillo in the dictator's day, Santo Domingo now — where military, fiscal, and commercial power is concentrated, where fortunes, deals, and decisions are made, where favours are peddled. In his heyday, Trujillo was estimated to be one of the richest men in the world; he instituted a form of state capitalism in which he was the state. The identification of political power with self-enrichment is fixed forever in the popular mind, and, indeed, it has hardly been disproved by the elected governments of the last thirty years.

Trujillo's death left the country floundering in uncertainties. It had no institutional structure to maintain it. Pressures from the United States, which feared then that the Cuban Revolution might spread to the Dominican Republic, led to the holding of democratic elections in December of 1962. Although Dominicans had only a sketchy understanding of what democracy meant, they elected a populist President, Juan Bosch, who promised sweeping social reforms and political freedom, even to the Communists. Those promises proved too much for the elite and the military, and nine months later Bosch was overthrown and exiled in a military coup. A junta ruled uneasily for eighteen months, until the constitutionalists rose in a popular surge against the military; they seemed almost on the point of defeating it when Lyndon Johnson ordered in the Marines, to quench what was the closest to a revolution that the people of the country had ever come. Elections were held again in 1966, and have been held every four years since.

My neighbours remain distrustful of democracy as they know it. A change of party in Samaná means a change of all official posts in the town, from governor to itinerant mailman, but apart from that the campesinos see little or no improvement in their lot. Some, embittered by the lack of opportunity and of paid work, turn their eyes elsewhere, but the majority fall back on the ingrained pattern, the preoccupation with finding food every day. Only the luck of the climate and the bounty of the soil have kept them from misery. As for democracy, their participation ends with the elections, for Dominican Presidents do not govern so much as rule by decree. In Samaná, the pattern still has not changed. We live at the end of the line, the receiving end of whatever may come from the capital — government decrees, price rises, shortages, delays — and everything makes us wary of life outside the peninsula. Although all my neighbours vote proudly on Election Day, dipping their index fingers in indelible ink to make sure they vote no more than once, they do not expect anything to change. They all tell stories of electoral frauds, vote buying, false counts, as though to insulate themselves against disappointment.

Although the Dominican Republic shares Hispaniola with Haiti, the landmass is virtually all that they do share. Dominicans harbour a deep prejudice against Haitians, an inherent racism that is seldom voiced but is pervasively present. It stems in part from the violence of their history — Dominicans never forget that it was from Haiti that they wrested their independence. And now that their country is considerably more developed than its threadbare neighbour, with a much higher per capita income, they do not welcome those Haitians who filter across the frontier, except as braceros, cane-cutters who work in conditions not far removed from slavery — a circumstance that has brought the Dominican Republic the censure of the United Nations Commission on Human Rights.

Of the many cruelties perpetrated by Trujillo, the most barbaric of all took place in October of 1937, when units of the Dominican Army, acting on a direct order from the dictator, hunted down and massacred between 15,000 and 20,000 Haitians — men, women, and children — in the Dominican provinces adjoining the frontier. The event was covered up at the time, and today Dominicans go silent when it is mentioned.

During Haiti's difficult years, when those who could, fled the country, it might have seemed that the simplest solution would have been for the Dominican government to open temporary refugee camps in its territory; but, with Dominican attitudes as unyielding as they are, it's not surprising that Haitians in their despair chose to chance the open sea rather than look toward the forbidding frontier to the east.

Dr Joaquín Balaguer began his political career in the thirties, as a loyal servant of Trujillo, in a variety of official posts and eventually as Trujillo's puppet

President — the post he occupied when Trujillo was assassinated. Balaguer's image could not be more different from that of his master — he is small, meek of manner, frail, soft-spoken, well known as a poet, scholar, and historian — yet, unscrupulous and politically astute, he has never strayed far from the exercise of power. He won the elections of 1966, which followed the American intervention, and governed steadily until 1978 — a period in which the country enjoyed a brief prosperity, thanks to a surge in sugar prices — and he returned to power in 1986, at the age of seventy-nine, and was reelected in a dubious election in 1990. He is now blind, yet his hold on power has been as tenacious as ever Trujillo's was, his mode of governing as autocratic, his use of patronage in government appointments as cunning, his command of the military as secure. He has used propaganda zealously, seeking to appear in the role of a benign grandfather who has given his entire life to his country. Yet nowadays, the length and breadth of the country, on the minibuses and in the market, you hear no good words for Balaguer — not even from those who voted for him. When I was last in the capital, you could read the same legend scrawled on corner after corner: '*Que se vaya ya!*' — 'Let him leave now!' And what brought discontent to a head was, as much as anything, the quincentenary.

When Balaguer was returned to office in 1986, he launched a vast programme of public building, mostly in the capital — construction projects that had a great deal to do with the appearance of the place and bore his name more often than not. It was as though Balaguer, in his last years in power, were bent on fulfilling in new concrete Trujillo's obsession with public self-enshrinement. He also had firmly in mind a project he was determined to carry through: the building of a huge lighthouse, the Faro a Colón, to commemorate Columbus's landing in 1492.

The idea of a lighthouse as a monument to Columbus's arrival was first put forth in the middle of the last century, and it stayed alive until, at the Fifth International American Conference, held in Santiago, Chile, in 1923, a resolution was passed to build such a lighthouse monument on the edge of Santo Domingo 'with the cooperation of the governments and peoples of America'. In 1929, an international competition was announced, with a prize of $10,000, for the design of such a shrine. The entries were sifted by a special commission, and in 1931 an international jury met in Madrid to study 455 submissions, from forty-eight countries. The award went, finally, to a young English architect, J. L. Gleave, who was still a student, and artists' impressions of his design for the Faro appeared in the Dominican press of the day. Time passed; then Trujillo took up the idea of the Faro with characteristic grandiloquence, planning a complex of buildings around the lighthouse, including a new Presidential palace for himself, and actually breaking ground for the project in April of 1948. The money promised by the other governments of Latin America was not forthcoming, however, and the Faro remained merely a plan. For Balaguer, however, the building of the Faro remained, from the years of the competition on, a matter of deep commitment: it was his destiny to build it, to bring it to completion. He bided his time, and in 1986 work on the Faro began in earnest. The quincentenary was six years away. There was no time to lose.

Over these past few years, I watched the Columbus Lighthouse lumber into being in the Parque del Este, on the east side of the Ozama River, looking across to the Colonial Quarter of Santo Domingo, and to the cathedral, where the lead casket with Columbus's remains lay, before being transferred to the finished lighthouse. At first, a forced clearing of the area around the site dismantled the shanty-towns and drove out about fifty thousand people, many of whom were given no promise of rehousing. On the bare, muddy expanse left by the bulldozers, the Faro began to rise.

We think of lighthouses as vertical towers that project a light horizontally, for ships to see. The Columbus Lighthouse, however, is a horizontal structure, like a recumbent beast, designed to throw its light vertically, upward. It has a long base and two stubby arms — the shape of a long cross or a short sword. Since it was clearly intended as one of the new wonders of the world, its scale is immense: it is nearly half a mile long; walls slant upward from each arm to meet at a point a hundred and twenty feet high, and are crowned with a beacon that is to project on the sky a lighted cross visible as far away as Puerto Rico, some two hundred miles east. It has the look of a concrete pyramid with one long extended arm: a humped, dinosaur look; an anonymous, inert greyness. Grass has now grown over the razed barrios, along with newly planted stands of trees bordering a web of new approach roads. At first sight, it has a curious effect on the eye, puzzling rather than impressive, and seems mournful and forbidding. You could easily believe that some huge, unnameable secret weapon was being assembled deep inside it. It puts me in mind more of Dr No than of Columbus.

Since Balaguer resumed the Presidency in August of 1990, things have been going very badly in the Dominican Republic. The elections were held that May, and we listened avidly to the first returns on the radio — the neighbours excitedly, for Juan Bosch appeared to be leading Balaguer. Suddenly, however, the electoral count was suspended, incomplete — nobody understood quite why. After a tense day or two, we were all back at work, while in the capital a bitter wrangling began. It lasted weeks, and finally, in mid-June, the electoral junta announced that Balaguer had won. Even so, the combined opposition votes exceeded his by half a million, making him very much a minority President. No one doubted that there had been electoral fraud. I knew of some in Samaná. Electoral fraud is not easy to bring off in our present political climate; for having done it, Balaguer did elicit some admiration. Those who had hoped that he might abandon his construction projects and give some attention to the backward state of the country's agriculture — which is to say, to the bare livelihood of those who lived outside the capital — were soon disenchanted; one of his first acts was to set in motion plans for the rapid completion of the Faro a Colón. That year was a drastic one for the campesinos, first in soaring prices of basic foods, and then in serious shortages of fuel and, of all things, sugar. The price of gasoline rose, and rose again. Perhaps even worse was the precarious state of the country's electrical grid, which occasioned nationwide daily electricity cuts, sometimes of twenty hours — cuts that played havoc with refrigeration, and with commerce in general. If there was hunger in the countryside, there was misery in the slums on the edges of the capital. Balaguer continued in Olympian indifference, unperturbed, deaf to dissent.

The ironies surrounding Balaguer's obsession with the Faro were ever more apparent. How much had the Faro cost to build? Twenty million dollars? A hundred million? People guess, but nobody will ever know, since Balaguer does not make public such accountings. Its light was to be the brightest in all the Americas, a stunning irony in a country whose electrical system is all but bankrupt. When the Faro is switched on, the campesinos said, the lights will go out in all the rest of the country. Besides, they remind you, sailors have no need of lighthouses anymore. And, they added, when he switched on the Faro, poor Balaguer wouldn't even be able to see the light.

I eavesdrop a lot on the long bus trips to Samaná,

and in 1992 the general talk always came around to the Faro, for it became, understandably, the incarnation of discontents, an object of concentrated scorn among the campesinos. At times, you heard the fervently expressed hope that when Balaguer pressed the button to switch on the Faro he would somehow be subsumed into it and projected skyward, and, with him, all politicians, to join Columbus in his Faro, because they've been doing to us the very thing that he did, haven't they, with rice now at five pesos a pound. It was not rage, however, that they directed toward the Faro — Dominicans, as they tell me often, are not good haters. They are too good-natured. Instead, they made the Faro into a national joke, a monument to absurdity — not just the absurdity of their own situation but the absurdity of all such monumentalizing, at a time when the world is more bent on tearing down shrines to the past than on building them. The five hundred years that the Faro was enshrining represented for the campesinos a very different history from that promulgated in the official publications of the quincentenary commission in Santo Domingo.

As it turned out, the inauguration of the Faro did not exactly fulfil Balaguer's lifelong dream; instead, it engendered a new respect for the *fucú* throughout the country. The world leaders who had been invited to attend the ceremony sent their excuses, to a man; the Pope, who was in the Dominican Republic to attend an ecumenical congress, pointedly absented himself. More poignantly, however, Balaguer's sister, his long companion, died the day before the event, and he himself could not be present. Although the Faro sends its light skyward at appointed hours, visitors mostly ignore it, and the people take the only revenge that is in their power by never mentioning it, by effectively forgetting its existence.

Balaguer's other interest in his policy of Dominican glorification has been, inevitably, tourism, and in the late eighties, especially, the country has seen a rash of hotel building and resort-making along the Caribbean coast, in the south, and on the wilder, Atlantic north coast, bringing with it all the furniture of tourist occupation, and all the expectations. It appears at first a very simple and agreeable proposition to those who live there: tourists come with money, and wish to stay, and so one must offer them something that will cause them to hand over some, if not all, of their money. It appeals to the young in the *aldeas* who have other ideas than trudging back and forth from the *conucos* all their lives. And it appealed enough to the first tourists so that the Dominican Republic has been turned into a kind of modern discovery, worthy of being called unspoiled.

Not for long, however. Already, two towns on the north coast have been overtaken by mass tourism and turned quickly into overcrowded, traffic-ridden nightmares. Huge projects, some of them bearing Columbus's name, have started up, foundered, and failed, leaving monumental arched gateways leading to wilderness. Restaurants open in hope and quite often close in disappointment. There is work, of course, in construction — 'building bars we can't afford to go into', as Orlando, the mason, likes to remark. We talk about tourism a lot by the stream, most seriously whenever there is a question of selling land. For a campesino to sell his land would mean money in the hand, something never known. But would the money in the hand last as the land lasts? In reality, the coming of tourism has made very little difference to the life of our *vecindad*, except for the occasional work it has offered in construction. It has, however, brought with it a great deal of *ilusión*, high hopes, great expectations.

Porfirio, who has a house above mine, by the road, a favourite meeting place in the neighbourhood, got a job as a foreman, building a small hotel in town — a good job, which gave him, after a year, enough to leave it and buy a black-and-white television set, and an automobile battery, which is recharged once a week. Every night now, the blue light flickers in Porfirio's house after sundown, and of an evening there will be thirty neighbours cross-legged in rows, transfixed but still talkative, with sleeping children among them. Sometimes I have gone up to see Porfirio and sat for a while, listening to the audience reaction. No matter what soap is sobbing its crisis on the screen, they are giving the drama only minimal attention. They point out the clothes, they crow at the food, they ogle the cars, they embrace the commercials. They are gazing through a window at a world they instantly want, and tourists are to them somehow emissaries from that world.

The inevitable discontents that are fuelled by the coming of tourists have led a lot of country people to leave behind them a life that, predictable though it is, gets harder rather than easier and holds out no hope of anything else. They may go to the capital, where they find that unemployment is chronic, prices are high, survival is much more precarious. Or they may take a more drastic course. In Samaná sometimes, on moonless nights, we will hear a boat pass, a boat of some power, but without lights. It is a *yola*, most likely — an open boat setting out with perhaps twenty people who have paid over most of their savings to the boatmaster to take them across the dangerous waters of the Mona Channel and land them, illegally, on a beach on the west shore of Puerto Rico. Some of the boats come to grief, and the sharks turn crossings into tragedies. Of those who land, some are caught at once, some later; but a good many filter in, an address in a pocket, are looked after at first by other Dominicans, then find work, hoping in time to send some money home and to save enough to make the flight to New York, untroubled by immigration, armed with more addresses, to find better work, eventually to become legal, with the dream of saving enough to set up a small *colmado* back in the *vecindad* they began in. One of the men from our neighbourhood went in a *yola*, worked in Puerto Rico for three months, was caught, and was returned by plane, his first flight. The fine he had to pay consumed all the money he had saved. We all turned out to welcome him back, however, and he has become something of a counsellor to others with *yolas* in mind. A nurse I know in town went in a *yola*, which was stopped about a mile out by the Dominican coast guard and turned back, the money confiscated (and later shared with the captain of the *yola*, she was sure). Every time I return to Samaná, there is an absence, a space: someone I know has gone in a *yola*.

In the Dominican Republic, Christmas and Easter are marked by the return, in flocks, of *Dominicanos ausentes* — those who live in the United States — on a visit to their pueblos, bearing gifts, wearing the gold chains and bright new clothes of success, and full of stories of colour and light, even if the chains, and possibly the roll of bills, have been borrowed for the occasion. The myth is perpetuated. I have spent considerable time explaining some of the complexities of that other world to my neighbours — things like paying for heat, which is incomprehensible to them. But it is a world they have come to want fiercely, even if only in the form of sneakers — simply, a better life. Over the last twenty years, there has been a Dominican diaspora that has taken almost a million out of the country.

I am by now used to the fatalism of my neighbours. It is a cheerful fatalism rather than a despairing one, mostly, although hopes and expectations are scarce. I know a good number of Dominicans, however, who are acutely aware of the situation in their country and have a clear view indeed of a possible future for it. Among them is a farmer, Gilberto, with whom I often talk, for he experiments indefatigably with new seeds that I bring him. I asked him last summer what he would like to see happen in his country.

He did not hesitate for a second. 'More than anything, I wish this country would lose its memory,' he said. 'We're still slaves of our own history — what happened to us is what we still expect to happen. I long to see the age of the *abuelos*, the grandfathers, Balaguer and Bosch, come to an end. Over thirty years, they have made it harder for those who live in the campo, never worse than now. I'd like to wipe out our present parties and politicians, all the corruption and patronage and secret deals, all the intrigue. I'd like to see an end to this weakness we have of always looking for a leader, a father — a grandfather, even — who will save us, who will make all our decisions for us, whom we can curse and grumble at. Our parties don't have programmes. All they do is parade their candidate for saviour, hoping enough of us will say, 'That's the man!' We need parties that put forward programmes, not saviours. We need young technocrats in the government who can come up with a national plan that will open up the country, give it work, and, most of all, *involve* us in our own country, give us some hope. I'd like to see all our children literate, our teachers and doctors paid decent salaries, the police, too, so that they didn't have to turn to crime. If only we modernized our agriculture, if we diversified from our sugar dependence, we could be the garden state of the Caribbean. We wouldn't need tourism to save us. Tourism is another kind of slavery for Dominicans.

Spaniards call tourism *putería* — whoring — and that's what it is, pleasing foreigners. It's corrupting, it's like a pollution. Take Samaná. If the government gave Samaná a million dollars for agricultural projects, well supervised, we could be exporting fruit and vegetables year-round, to other islands, to Florida, and living well. We could have solar energy and irrigation systems and crops year-round. Instead, they talk of a golf course. Can you imagine what an insult it is to us, who have always lived from the land, to put down a golf course among us? Or to build that monstrous monument to Columbus? As far as I'm concerned, Columbus didn't so much discover America as bring into being the Third World.'

Samaná, at the end of the line, has always had a trickle of tourists, but its facilities are still frail and few. The place survives, however, on rumours of imminent prosperity; and while many of its projects have foundered, some are coming to fruition. At the moment, the place lives in a kind of limbo of possibilities, and the *chisme* this year has been a little headier than usual. The mayor of Miami made a visit, in 1991, expressed his undying love for Samaná, and promised to send a consignment of used official cars from Miami, which have so far not arrived. A group of conservationists has been taking a growing interest in Samaná for the last three years, and a plan is afoot to have the bay and the peninsula declared a Biosphere Reserve, to maintain the native species, including the manatee, to prevent pollution of the bay, and to protect the habitat of the humpback whales that spend their breeding time in the bay from late January until early March every year, before their migration north. It has not been easy for me to explain to the neighbours just what a Biosphere Reserve means, or would mean to them. They are mystified by the notion; I think they see themselves as having to dress up as Tainos.

Most of the *chisme*, however, surrounded the opening of a luxury hotel, on an outcrop of rocky coast overlooking the beach at Las Flechas and facing the little island of Cayo Levantado. The hotel took shape in fits and starts for three years, and a number of men from our neighbourhood worked on it at various times. It is built in James Bond Caribbean: red roofs, verandas, palms wild and potted, a private force of uniformed guards, and a tariff that, if the *chisme* is close, sets everyone's eyes rolling. About a quarter of a mile from the hotel sits the small town of Los Cacaos, hugging the beach and sprawling up the slope — a jaunty, easygoing, raucous community of people, who are quite fired up by the sudden transformation of their coast. If any one of the inhabitants of Los Cacaos had in hand what a guest pays to sleep a night in the hotel, he would instantly be among the richest in town. Tourists, as a rule, want to go shopping; and shopping in the town of Samaná offers the slimmest of pickings. There is the market, where goats' throats are often cut in public; there is a hardware store like an Aladdin's cave; there are vendors of hats made of varnished palm leaves; and there are three shoeshine boys who stare gloomily at tourist sandals. But there is not much more except for the roar of motorcycles, the main attainable dream of young Dominicans. I cannot think that much good can come from placing two such disparate groups, so far apart economically, in such sudden proximity. At best, they trouble each other; and certainly the hotel's presence feeds local discontents, when people at scarcely survival level live in such an opulent shadow. They fear that very soon their own beaches will be closed to them, as has begun to happen, and, worse, that they may be forced to move — to yield up their land to the needs of tourism — by government decree. The tourist enterprises that have been successful in the Dominican Republic are those in which the tourists are enclosed in vast, caged, patrolled compounds, the concentration camps of leisure, with Dominican workers shipped in during the day and out at night. The fence makes sense. The division is dire. Besides, after the first flush of construction tourism does not bring the abundance of work it initially seems to promise. The revenues do not filter down in any noticeable way to the local inhabitants. I would not be surprised to see some local merry men form a latter-day Robin Hood band, swooping down from the palm trees and turning Samaná into a tropical version of Sherwood Forest.

Simultaneously, however, another future hovers over Samaná. In October of 1990, the Dominican government signed an agreement with an American-owned company called Once Once, S.A., granting it the right to explore for oil in certain parts of the country, among them Samaná Bay. While it is difficult to see how the place might become a tourist mecca, a Biosphere Reserve, and a centre for oil exploration all at once, such considerations are of little concern to Balaguer, who will not be around to face the consequences. Nor do my neighbours show much alarm or consternation at these prospects. Whatever may come to pass, it will happen to them as it happened to the Tainos, without any regard for their preferences; it has become their nature to accept rather than want. They gaze at the cruise ships that nose into Samaná Bay with the same wary eyes, the same unease, with which the Indians watched the coming of the caravels.

Columbus's first voyage is by now a matter more of legend than of history; but two scholars, Dr J.L. Montalvo Guenard, in a thesis published in Puerto Rico in 1933, and the Dominican historian Bernardo Vega, in a recent paper, have, from a close reading of the text of the journal, made a strong case for Columbus's Samaná landfall taking place not on the beach of Las Flechas but at Rincón, at the far end of the peninsula. They have convinced me; but it is unlikely that the history books will be revised. I tried to explain this quibble to Pucho, but he only looked at me with a mixture of scorn and alarm that I could find nothing better to do with my time. The idea that the new hotel may be founded on a historical misplacement tickles him, however.

It seems to me salutary that some serious arguments over Columbus and the Spanish Conquest arose as they did at this precise stage in our global history, since they raise disturbing questions about the meanings and evaluations of the past — questions that matter not to historians alone. We live in a postcolonial world, and we have, in our time, grown steadily more adamant about human rights, more sensitive to their violation. It seems to me that this must inevitably affect our reading and reassessment of history. It is why we gravitate to seeing the conquest through the eyes of Las Casas rather than those of Columbus, and why we are grateful for his clarity, his humanity, and his indignation. We may argue about human rights, for they are, in a sense, abstractions, but we do not argue about human wrongs. We recognize them physically; we can point to them, in the past as in the present. Shame and indignation are our measures, as they were to Las Casas. Confronting human wrongs is our common cause at present. About the wrongs of the past we can do nothing, but we can at least look at them squarely, and see them clearly.

Fictions

Many writers trudge through my attention, some of them passing fancies only, some becoming lifelong friends, and some unfailing reminders of the wonders and complexities of putting-into-words. I read other writers with an extra antenna out, taking in not just what is said, but also how, watching what the words do. Just occasionally, however, the work of a single writer will take possession of my whole awareness, bringing an unexpected light.

The writer who has most caused in me the vertigo of realization has unquestionably been Jorge Luis Borges. I first read him in the fifties, and went on to translate him for an English edition of his most celebrated volume, *Ficciones.* I met him in 1964, in Buenos Aires, when he was already blind, and maintained a friendship with him until he died in 1986. We met in different parts of the world, and had many long conversations, about writers and writing, and very often about language itself. Over the years I have translated a fair amount of his poetry; and I have never stopped rereading him, finding that mischievous, elusive wavelength, hearing that soft, ironic voice in my head.

I found at once with Borges a coincidence of mind,

not simply an enthusiasm for his writings, but more, a complete accord with the view of language implied in all his writing, a view he would often enlarge on in conversation. Borges referred to all his writings — essays, stories, poems, reviews — as fictions. He never propounded any particular theory of fictions, yet it is the key to his particular lucid, keen, and ironic view of existence. To make his thinking on the matter as clear as I can, I will put it in the form of precepts:

*

A fiction is any construct of language — a story, an explanation, a plan, a theory, a dogma — that gives a certain shape to reality.

Reality, that which is beyond language, functions by mainly indecipherable laws, which we do not understand, and over which we have limited control. To give some form to reality, we bring into being a variety of fictions.

A fiction, it is understood, can never be true, since the nature of language is utterly different from the nature of reality.

A fiction is not to be confused with a hypothesis, which poses a fiction as a truth and attempts to verify it from the reality.

A fiction is intended principally to be useful, to be serviceable, to be appropriate, to make some kind of sense of reality.

Fictions bring things to order for the time being only. Given a shifting reality, they have constantly to be remade.

We are physical beings, rooted in the physical cycle of life-and-death. Yet we are also users of language, fiction-makers, and language and fictions are not, like us, subject to natural laws. Through them, we are able to cross over into a timeless dimension, to bring into being alternate worlds, to enjoy the full freedom of the imaginable.

Language itself is an irony — while we use it to create systems and formulations that are intelligible, coherent, and permanent, the reality they purport to put in order remains shifting, changeable, and chaotic, making it necessary for us all the time to revise our fictions, to dissolve and re-form them.

We are capable of generating the fiction of immortality, yet it in no way exempts us from death.

A book is an irony, mocking the person who writes it. By making his fiction out of language, the writer moves it into a timeless dimension, while he must remain rooted in time.

Our larger fictions — social theories, political systems, the idea of a Supreme Being — are not inherently true but are sustained for a time by belief. Most of them eventually outlive their usefulness.

Works of literature are reliable fictions, our fictions of enlightenment, our solace. Poetry and prose are merely different modes of fictions, poetry attempting to move closer to experience as a happening, prose maintaining a certain lucid distance.

The most common of all confusions is to imagine that we have changed reality when all we have done is to alter our fiction of it.

It is crucial never to lose the sense that our fictions are in fact fictions, even while appreciating their usefulness, and suspending our disbelief when we choose to.

Reality is given to us: making fictions of it is in large part what we do with it.

We are all *ficcioneros*, inveterate fiction-makers — it is through our fictions, private and public, that we make sense of our world, and find some equilibrium in it, it is through our fictions that we create ourselves.

*

These words are in no sense Borges's — he did not philosophize, considering philosophy simply another branch of the fantastic and the fictional — but they are more or less the bones of his thinking about language and literature. In Borges's universe, in our universe, there is no single truth, there are only multitudes of fictions; and we have to choose amongst them, to find those that fit us. More than anything, we continue to make our own. Making fictions out of what happens is an activity, a constant self-creation. We enfable our daily existence.

I found this to be true among my neighbours in the Dominican Republic, most of them illiterate. They lived by the stories they made out of their days, by the imaginative explanations they invented for things beyond their ken. They had no archives beyond a series of polished anecdotes; and when they told the stories of their lives, their lives varied with each telling. In their shared fictions lay their morality, their way of surviving. In their imagination lay their strength.

We live within an intricate web of fictions — the fictions of daily gossip, the fictions of a profession or a career, newspaper fictions, the fictions of writers and communicators, the fictions of entertainment, the fictions of politics, the fictions of nationality — out of which we fashion a quilt of chosen fictions, a set that suits us — fictions of our childhood, of pieces of our past, fictions of our loves and our losses, fictions of the whole web of our lives. We constantly tell ourselves stories, dividing the continuum of our lives into tellable segments, each with a conclusion.

Language, however, is a slippery and sometimes treacherous element, and can glibly stray from the reality it is meant to deal with. It is for that reason that we have to take great care over the act of putting-into-words, the fashioning of our fictions. At best, it is an act of creation, part astonishment, part invention, part wisdom.

Perhaps our fictions, if they find their way appropriately into words, ironically, are the most durable thing about us.

POEMS I

Scotland

It was a day peculiar to this piece of the planet,
when larks rose on long thin strings of singing
and the air shifted with the shimmer of actual angels.
Greenness entered the body. The grasses
shivered with presences, and sunlight
stayed like a halo on hair and heather and hills.
Walking into town, I saw, in a radiant raincoat,
the woman from the fish-shop. 'What a day it is!'
cried I, like a sunstruck madman.
And what did she have to say for it?
Her brow grew bleak, her ancestors raged in their
                                                    graves
as she spoke with their ancient misery:
'We'll pay for it, we'll pay for it, we'll pay for it.'

The Spiral

The seasons of this year are in my luggage.
Now, lifting the last picture from the wall,
I close the eyes of the room. Each footfall
clatters on the bareness of the stair.
The family ghosts fade in the hanging air.
Mirrors reflect the silence. There is no message.
I wait in the still hall for a car to come.
Behind, the house will dwindle to a name.

Places, addresses, faces left behind.
The present is a devious wind

obliterating days and promises.
Tomorrow is a tinker's guess.
Marooned in cities, dreaming of greenness,
or dazed by journeys, dreading to arrive—
change, change is where I live.

For possibility,
I choose to leave behind
each language, each country.
Will this place be an end,
or will there be one other,
truer, rarer?

Often now, in dream,
abandoned landscapes come,
figuring a constant theme:
Have you left us behind?
What have you still to find?

Across the spiral distance,
through time and turbulence,
the rooted self in me
maps out its true country.

And, as my father found
his own small weathered island,
so will I come to ground

where that small man, my son,
can put his years on.

For him, too, time will turn.

Daedalus

My son has birds in his head.

I know them now. I catch
the pitch of their calls, their shrill
cacophonies, their chitterings, their coos.
They hover behind his eyes and come to rest
on a branch, on a book, grow still,
claws curled, wings furled.
His is a bird world.

I learn the flutter of his moods,
his moments of swoop and soar.
From the ground I feel him try
the limits of the air—
sudden lift, sudden terror—
and move in time to cradle
his quivering, feathered fear.

At evening, in the tower,
I see him to sleep and see
the hooding-over of eyes,
the slow folding of wings.
I wake to his morning twitterings,
to the *croomb* of his becoming.

He chooses his selves — wren, hawk,
swallow or owl — to explore
the trees and rooftops of his heady wishing.
Tomtit, birdwit.
Am I to call him down, to give him

a grounding, teach him gravity?
Gently, gently.
Time tells us what we weigh, and soon enough
his feet will reach the ground.
Age, like a cage, will enclose him.
So the wise men said.

My son has birds in his head.

My Father, Dying

At summer's succulent end,
the house is green-stained.
I reach for my father's hand

and study his ancient nails.
Feeble-bodied, yet at intervals
a sweetness appears and prevails.

The heavy-scented night
seems to get at his throat.
It is as if the dark coughed.

In the other rooms of the house,
the furniture stands mumchance.
Age has graved his face.

Cradling his wagged-out chin,
I shave him, feeling bone
stretching the waxed skin.

By his bed, the newspaper lies furled.
He has grown too old
to unfold the world,

which has dwindled to the size of a sheet.
His room has a stillness to it.
I do not call it waiting, but I wait,

anxious in the dark, to see if
the butterfly of his breath
has fluttered clear of death.

There is so much might be said,
dear old man, before I find you dead;
but we have become too separate

now in human time
to unravel all the interim
as your memory goes numb.

But there is no need for you to tell—
no words, no wise counsel,
no talk of dying well.

We have become mostly hands
and voices in your understanding.
The whole household is pending.

I am not ready
to be without your frail and wasted body,
your miscellaneous mind-way,

the faltering vein of your life.
Each evening, I am loth
to leave you to your death.

Nor will I dwell on
the endless, cumulative question
I ask, being your son.

But on any one
of these nights soon,
the dark for you will not crack with dawn,

and then I will begin
with you that hesitant conversation
going on and on and on.

Once at Piertarvit

Once at Piertarvit,
one day in April,
the edge of spring,
with the air a-ripple
and sea like knitting,
as Avril and Ann
and Ian and I
walked in the wind
along the headland,
Ian threw an apple
high over Piertarvit.

Not a great throw,
you would say, if you'd seen it,
but good for Ian.
His body tautened,

his arm let go
like a flesh-and-bone bow,
and the hard brown apple
left over from autumn
flew up and up,
crossing our gaze,
from the cliff at Piertarvit.

Then all at once, horror
glanced off our eyes,
Ann's, mine, Avril's.
As the apple curved
in the stippled sky,
at the top of its arc,
it suddenly struck
the shape of a bird,
a gull that had glided
down from nowhere
above Piertarvit.

We imagined the thud
and the thin ribs breaking,
blood, and the bird
hurtling downwards.
No such thing.
The broad wings wavered
a moment only,
then air sustained them.
The gull glided on
while the apple fell
in the sea at Piertarvit.

Nobody spoke.
Nobody whistled.
In that one moment,
our world had shifted.
The four of us stood
stock-still with awe
till, breaking the spell,
Ian walked away
with a whirl in his head.
The whole sky curdled
over Piertarvit.

I followed slowly,
with Ann and Avril
trailing behind.
We had lost our lightness.
Even today,
old as I am,
I find it hard
to say, without wonder,
'Ian hit a bird
with an apple, in April,
once at Piertarvit.'

The Manse

The house that shored my childhood up
razed to the ground? I stood, amazed,
gawking at a block of air,
unremarkable except

I had hung it once with crazy
daywish and nightmare.

Expecting to pass a wistful
indulgent morning, I had sprung the gate.
Facing me was a wood
between which and myself
a whole crow-gabled and slated
mythology should have stood.

No room now for the rambling
wry remembering I had planned;
nor could I replant
that plot with a second childhood.
Luck, to have been handed
instead a forgettable element,

and not to have had to meet
regretful ghosts in rooms of glass.
That house by now is fairytale
and I can gloss it over
as easily as passing
clear through a wall.

Galilea

Bleached white, bedazzled
by the bright light falling,
the hilltop holds me up.
Below, the coastline bares its teeth.

Winded, burned to the bone, between
the stony green of the olive,
the grey grimace of stone,
I look dazedly down.

How to come to rest
in this raw, whittled landscape
where earth, air, fire, and water
bluntly demand obeisance?

Perhaps to fix one place
in a shifting world where time
talks and where too many selves
criss-cross and demand
enactment and re-enactment,

somewhere decent to die in,
somewhere which could become
landscape and vocabulary,
equilibrium, home.

James Bottle's Year

December finds him
outside, looking skyward.
The year gets a swearword.

His rage is never permanent.
By January he's out,
silent and plough-bent.

All white February,
he's in a fury
of wind-grief and ground-worry.

By March, he's back
scouring the ground for luck,
for rabbit-run and deer-track.

April is all sounds and smiles.
The hill is soft with animals.
His arms describe miles.

The local girls say
he's honeyed and bee-headed
at haytime in May.

In June,
he'll stay up late, he'll moon
and talk to children.

No one sees him in July.
At dawn, he'll ride away
with distance in his eye.

In August, you'd assume
yourself to be almost welcome.
He keeps open time.

But, on one September morning,
you'll see cloud-worries form.
His eyes flash storm warnings.

October is difficult.
He tries to puzzle out
if it's his or the season's fault.

In November, he keeps still
through hail and snowfall,
thinking through it all.

What's causing the odd weather?
Himself, or the capricious air?
Or the two together?

December, breathing hard,
he's back outside, hurling skyward
his same swearword.

In Such a Poise Is Love

Why should a hint of winter
shadow the window while the insects enter,
or a feel of snowfall, taking corners off
the rough wall and the roof,
while the sun, hanging in the sky,
hotly denies its contrary?

As if it knew all future must entail
probable tempered by improbable,
so the mind wanders to the unforeseen,
and the eye, waking, poises between
shock and recognition — the clothes, the chair,
bewildering, familiar.

In such a poise is love. But who
can keep the balance true,
can stay in the day's surprise, moving

between twin fears, of losing and of having?
Who has not, in love's fever,
insisted on the fatal vow, 'for ever',
and sensed, before the words are gone,
the doom in them dawn?

A Lesson for Beautiful Women

Gazing and gazing in the glass,
she might have noticed slow cotillions pass
and might have seen
a blur of others in the antique green.
Transfixed instead,
she learned the inclinations of her neat small head
and, startling her own surprise,
wondered at the wonder in her jewelled eyes.

Gardens of rainbow and russet might have caught her
but, leaning over goldfish water,
she watched the red carp emphasise her mouth,
saw underneath
the long green weeds lace in
through a transparency of face and skin,
smiled at herself smiling reflectively,
lending a new complexion to the sky.

In service to her beauty
long mornings lengthened to a duty
patiently served before the triple mirror
whose six eyes sent her many a time in terror

to hide in rows of whispering dresses;
but her glass soul her own three goddesses
pursued, and if she turned away,
the same three mouths would breathe 'Obey, obey!'

And in procession, young men princely came,
ambassadors to her cool perfect kingdom.
Set at a distance by their praise,
she watched their unspeaking eyes adore her face.
Inside, her still self waited. Nothing moved.
Finally, by three husbands richly loved
(none of them young), she drifted into death,
the glass clouding with her last moist breath.

Changed into legend, she was given rest;
and, left alone at last,
the small mim servant shuttered in her being
peeped mousily out; and seeing
the imperious mirrors glazed and still,
whimpered forlornly down the dark hall
'Oh, grieve for my body, who would not let me be.
She, not I, was a most beautiful lady.'

Calenture

He never lives to tell,
but other men bring back the tale

of how, after days of gazing at the sea
unfolding itself incessantly and greenly—

hillsides of water crested with clouds of foam—
he, heavy with a fading dream of home,
clambers aloft one morning and, looking down,
cries out at seeing a different green—
farms, woods, grasslands, an extending plain,
hazy meadows, a long tree-fledged horizon,
his ship riding deep in rippled grain,
swallows flashing in the halcyon sun,
the road well-known to him, the house, the garden,
figures at the gate — and, foundering in his passion,
he suddenly climbs down and begins to run.
Dazed by his joy, the others watch him drown.

Such calenture, they say,
is not unknown in lovers long at sea

yet such a like fever did she make in me
this green-leaved summer morning, that I,
seeing her confirm a wish made lovingly,
felt gate, trees, grass, birds, garden glimmer over,
a ripple cross her face, the sky quiver,
the cropped lawn sway in waves, the house founder,
the light break into flecks, the path shimmer
till, finding her eyes clear and true at the centre,
I walked toward her on the flowering water.

For Her Sake

Her world is all aware. She reads
omens in small happenings, the fall of a teaspoon,

flurries of birds, a cat's back arching,
words unspoken, wine spilt.
She will notice moods in handwriting,
be tuned to feelings in a room,
sense ill luck in a house, take heed of ghosts,
hear children cry before the sound has reached her,
stay unperturbed in storms, keep silence
where speech would spoil. Days are her changes,
weather her time.

Whether it be becalmed in cool mornings
of air and water, or thunderstruck through nights
where flesh craves and is answered, in her, love
knows no division, is an incarnation
of all her wonder, as she makes
madness subside, and all thought-splintered things
grow whole again.

Look below. She walks in the garden,
preoccupied with paths, head bent,
beautiful, not at rest, as objects are,
but moving, in the fleck of light and shade.
Her ways are hers, not mine. Pointless to make
my sense of her, or claim her faithfulness.
She is as women are, aware
of her own mystery, in her way faithful
to flowers and days; and from the window's distance,
I watch her, haunted by her otherness.

Well to love true women, whose whims are wise,
whose world is warm, whose home is time,

and well to pleasure them, since, last of all,
they are the truth which men must tell,
and in their pleasure, houses lighten,
gardens grow fruitful, and true tales are told.
Well to move from mind's distance
into their aura, where the air
is shifting, intimate, particular.

And of true women, she, whose eyes illumine
this day I wake in — well to mark
her weather, how her look is candid,
her voice clear-toned, her heart private,
her love both wild and reticent.
Well to praise and please her, well to make
this for her sake.

Outlook, Uncertain

No season
brings conclusion.

Each year,
through heartache, nightmare,

true loves alter,
marriages falter,

and lovers illumine
the antique design,

apart, together,
foolish as weather,

right as rain,
sure as ruin.

Must you, then, and I
adjust the whole sky

over every morning?
Or else, submitting

to cloud and storm,
enact the same

lugubrious ending,
new lives pending?

The Figures on the Frieze

Darkness wears off and, dawning into light,
they find themselves unmagically together.
He sees the stains of morning in her face.
She shivers, distant in his bitter weather.

Diminishing of legend sets him brooding.
Great goddess-figures conjured from his book
blur what he sees with bafflement of wishing.
Sulky, she feels his fierce, accusing look.

Familiar as her own, his body's landscape
seems harsh and dull to her habitual eyes.

Mystery leaves, and, mercilessly flying,
the blind fiends come, emboldened by her cries.

Avoiding simple reach of hand for hand
(which would surrender pride) by noon they stand
withdrawn from touch, reproachfully alone,
small in each other's eyes, tall in their own.

Wild with their misery, they entangle now
in baffling agonies of why and how.
Afternoon glimmers, and they wound anew,
flesh, nerve, bone, gristle in each other's view.

'What have you done to me?' From each proud heart,
new phantoms walk in the deceiving air.
As the light fails, each is consumed apart,
he by his ogre vision, she by her fire.

When night falls, out of a despair of daylight,
they strike the lying attitudes of love,
and through the perturbations of their bodies,
each feels the amazing, murderous legends move.

Me to You

I

Summer's gone brown and, with it,
our wanderings in the shires, our ways.
Look at us now.

A shuttered house drips in Moroccan rain.
A mill sits ghostly in the green of France.

Beaches are empty now of all but pebbles.
But still, at crossroads, in senorial gardens,
we meet, sleep, wrangle, part, meet, part,
making a lodging of the heart.

Now that the sea begins to dull with winter,
and I so far, and you so far
(and home further than either),
write me a long letter,
as if from home.

              Tell me about the snowfalls
at night, and tell me how we'd sit in firelight,
hearing dogs huff in sleep, hearing the geese
hiss in the barn, hearing the horse clop home.
Say how the waterfall sounds, and how the weeds
trail in the slithering river.
Write me about the weather.

Perhaps
a letter across water,
something like this, but better,
would almost move us strangely
closer to home.

Write, and I'll come.

All day I have been writing you a letter.

Now, after hours of gazing at the page
and watching the screen of rain, I have enacted

a flow of endless letters in my head
(all of them different) and not one
in any written shape to send.
Those letters never end.

In between pages of wishing, I walked to the river
and wrote you of how the water
wrinkles and eddies and wanders away.
That was easier to say.

I wrote of how the snow
had fallen and turned blue,
and how the bush you wanted
could not be planted.

Some pages were all remembering — the places,
faces, frontiers, rooms, and days we went through
ages ago.
(Do you do this too?)
Always coming back to snow.

Mostly an endless, useless run of questions.
How are you now? How is it there?
Who will you and I
be in a year?
Who are we now?

Oh no,
there is no letter to send you, only this stream
of disconnected brooding, this rhythm
of wanting, cumbersome
in words, lame.

Come.

Remembering Robert Graves

Had he lived, Robert Graves would have been a hundred years old in July of 1985; as it happened, he died at ninety, in November of 1985, in the village of Deyá, on the rocky northwestern coast of Majorca, where he had made his home for half of his long life, and where I first met him, in the summer of 1953. We enjoyed a close friendship, in the form of an endless conversation, until it was abruptly and irretrievably severed in 1961. Very seldom do I think of those years, but I was considerably formed and changed by them. With the centenary, Graves's name was very much in the air, with three biographies, a documentary film, an endearing memoir of him by his son William, symposia on his work, and an act of homage by the Majorcan government. Carcanet Press, in Britain, is to reprint most of his work — an eight-year project, since he published more than a hundred and thirty books in his lifetime. His life and his writings so interact that they cannot be unravelled: writing was how he lived.

The English have always kept Graves at a distance, as if he were an offshore island, out of the mainstream — something they quite often do with English writers who choose to live elsewhere and are still successful.

Even so, he is now firmly lodged in literary history, and critics may write of him without incurring one of his famously withering broadsides. Those who know his work well probably think first of his poetry; many people, however, know his name only from the television version of *I, Claudius*. Generally, the book of his that first springs to mind is *Good-bye to All That,* the autobiography he produced in 1929, out of a time of great personal stress.

Never was a title more fervently meant: as he put it, the book dealt with 'what I was, not what I am'. Its tone is one of blunt irreverence; by writing it, he was shedding his past, and turning his back on England and what he saw as the hypocrisy of its values and public institutions. He wrote it as one who had survived the tyrannies of conventional schooling and the dehumanizing horrors of the trenches, and no book of his did more to imprint his name on the attention of the public. He fled England just before it was published, leaving behind him a past he had chosen to renounce, even though he had already been irrevocably formed by it.

Graves had an Irish father, a German mother, a Scottish grandmother, a patrician English upbringing, a Welsh predilection, and a classical education. His whole personality formed itself from a mass of oppositions, of contraries. His father, a minor poet and a celebrated writer of Irish songs, worked as a school inspector in London. A widower left with five children to look after, he remarried, in 1891, a grandniece of the German historian Leopold von Ranke, and this genetic connection was one that Graves often invoked. Narrow-minded and pious both, his mother imposed a stern morality on her husband and children, and saddled Robert with a moral scrupulousness that left him socially inept and ill-prepared for the rigours of an English public school. In 1909, Graves was sent to Charterhouse, where his middle name, von Ranke, occasioned general derision, even outright persecution, as did his piety and his priggishness about sex. Although studies were not fashionable at Charterhouse, he took refuge in them. He left school just as the First World War was breaking out, and some ten days later he enlisted with a commission in the Royal Welsh Fusiliers. Not yet twenty, he was in France, and at the front, amid the running horror of death and decay every fearful day. In July, 1916, at the beginning of the Somme offensive, Graves was wounded by shrapnel, four days before he turned twenty-one; shortly afterward, the notice of his death from wounds appeared in the London *Times*.

He talked to me often about the war. My father had been wounded in the same battle: my mother kept in a small box the bullet that had been taken from his lung; I could scarcely hold it. Graves told me once that he considered himself exceptionally lucky in knowing that nothing that happened to him afterward could ever match the horror that he had gone through in the trenches.

The war left Graves in a precarious state, shell-shocked and suffering from severe war neurosis. It was during this time that Graves, accompanying his close friend Siegfried Sassoon to neurasthenic treatment, met the presiding physician, Dr W.H.R. Rivers, who had once been an anthropologist and was now a neurologist. After the war, Graves continued to visit him in Cambridge, where Rivers was a professor. Rivers planted in Graves's mind an interest in matriarchal societies and woman rule, which would later find fuller expression in his controversial work *The White Goddess*. More immediately, Rivers made Graves see that his cure was in writing: that the unconscious was the source not only of his nightmares but also of his creativity. He urged Graves to use his poetry to explore his pain. I think Rivers did more than anyone to show Graves just how his life and art were essentially connected. From that time on, Graves wrote whenever he could, wherever he was, convinced that in poetry lay a hope of sanity but at the same time suspecting that his 'insanity' made his poetry possible: were he to be entirely sane, his creativity might dry up. He needed his madness, his nerve. The poetry was in the pain.

While Graves was still in the Army, he abruptly proposed marriage, after short acquaintance, to Nancy Nicholson, then eighteen, sister of Ben Nicholson, the painter. She had strong feminist opinions for her day and refused to assume the married name of Graves (her two girls bore the Nicholson surname, her two boys that of Graves). Now a civilian and without qualifications or money, Graves elected to go to Oxford and eventually read for a degree in literature in the hope that it might lead to a teaching post. Money remained a recurring problem, although he and Nancy were full of plans as to how to earn it.

They were mired in domesticity; he shopped, cooked, washed, attended to the children, and wrote furiously all the time. By now he and Nancy had become more comrades than lovers, joined in a constant money worry. Enthralled by some poems of a young American poet he had read in *The Fugitive*, Graves had begun to correspond with their author, Laura Riding. They exchanged literary opinions, and Graves, impressed by her intelligence and her near-belligerent confidence, invited her to join Nancy and him to work with them. She arrived in England in early 1926, and for the next thirteen years she was to dominate Graves's existence, to prove his nemesis.

*

Laura Riding's influence on those who knew her owes more to her emphatic presence than to her writings, although it would have meant death to say it to her. I have known seven people who were close to her during her time with Graves, and something of the same dazed and faraway look came into their eyes whenever they spoke of her. Certain of her own supreme worth and intelligence, certain that her poetry was bringing a new clarity to language, Riding felt her work had been too sparsely appreciated at home, and she accepted Graves's invitation, hoping to find in Europe some like-minded souls. Graves had accepted a post lecturing on English literature in Cairo, and a week after her arrival in England Laura embarked for Egypt with the entire family, who already regarded her as an essential presence. The stay in Egypt proved less than fruitful, and after four months Graves resigned, and sailed, with the family, back to England. He was entranced by Laura. Where Graves wrestled with dualities, Laura was single-mindedly certain. The ferocity of her judgments occasionally verged on cruelty. To Graves, she was at once a demanding mentor, a clarifier, and a stimulating collaborator, utterly without doubts. He was also deeply in love with her. At first, he and Laura and Nancy declared themselves The Trinity and lived together. Soon, however, he moved to London to work there with Laura. Graves saw Laura's coming into his life, through poetry, as a magical event; he could do nothing but accept it.

The continuing story of Robert and Laura is a turbulent one, often painful, sometimes touching the edge of madness. Graves bore it stoically: the break with Nancy and the children, a rival for Laura's affections, her suicide leap from an upper window and her convalescence. In October of 1929, he and Laura left England behind, and made their way eventually to Majorca. The success of *Good-bye to All That* had shown Graves a way to survive as a poet. He said often that he bred show dogs in order to be able to afford a cat. The dogs were prose; the cat was poetry. Thanks to his show dogs, he was able to buy land and build a house, and to start up with Laura a small colony of clarity and literary industry in Deyá, which she ruled by will and whim. Graves now gave way to her entirely, declaring her work far above his. In 1933, he wrote the two Claudius novels, and they came out to great acclaim the following year. Laura disparaged them, although they were the source of all funds; he begged his friends never to mention any of his work in front of her, and in new publishing contracts he insisted that a work of hers be published along with his. He discussed endlessly with Laura his growing interest in goddess worship. To it she added the vehemence of her own ideas, and soon she became to Graves not simply critic and mentor and lover and poet but muse. Later, she claimed to have been the source of all Graves's notions of poetry as goddess worship. She was not. She was much more: she was their incarnation.

By 1936, the Spanish Civil War was looming and, as foreign residents, Robert and Laura were given the choice of leaving immediately on a British destroyer from Palma, the capital of Majorca, or remaining to take their chances on an island that had shown itself to be predominantly pro-Franco. They left, and the Spanish frontier closed behind them. Although Graves went back to England, it was no longer his country. Any return to Spain seemed unlikely, war in Europe being nearly inevitable. The couple felt themselves fugitives, refugees; relations between them had grown more distant, although Graves remained unswervingly loyal to Laura. A sign came in the form of an adulatory mention of her poems in *Time* by one Schuyler Jackson, a friend of a friend of Graves. Intrigued, Laura abruptly decided to return to America; arrangements were made, and Graves found himself in early 1939 accompanying her to Bucks County, Pennsylvania, where the Jacksons had a farm. Again, events took several savage turns. Laura assumed what she considered her rightful place at the centre of the magic circle, and took upon herself the rearranging of the lives around her. Jackson's wife was declared a witch and driven to breakdown. Graves was given his notice as collaborator and champion. She and Jackson were eventually to marry and move to Florida. Broken in spirit, Graves returned to England just as war was breaking out in Europe.

Graves never saw Laura again, yet he remained forever mesmerized by her: if her name came up in conversation, he would frequently go silent, slipping into a trance of memory. His rejection by Laura had wounded him deeply, but he refused to speak ill of her. In any case, he had found refuge in a new love. Alan Hodge, then a young poet and later Graves's valued collaborator, had brought his young wife, Beryl, into the circle, and they followed Laura and Robert to America. As the dramas unfolded, Robert found in Beryl's company a quiet, cool sanity that he badly needed, and a devotion to which he was not slow to respond. With Alan Hodge's eventual blessing, Beryl joined Robert in England, and she never left him.

War had broken out, uncertainties loomed, but Graves settled down with Beryl in the Devon countryside, and for the next six years he poured out work — writing poems, producing historical novels for which he did prodigious reading, and collaborating with Alan Hodge on a crisp, eminently sensible, and often humorous study of English prose style, called *The Reader Over Your Shoulder*, the most useful of all his books, as he said. His life with Beryl was calm and sustaining; it was also spiced by her humour — something Graves had not enjoyed for some time.

*

Graves has described how, at his desk in early 1944, he felt a sudden surge of illumination, and began feverishly writing the manuscript that was to be published as *The White Goddess*. Subtitled *A Historical Grammar of Poetic Myth*, it was to become a sacred book to a fair number of poets, and to enjoy a great vogue in the sixties, though more as a 'magic' book than as a brilliantly argued synthesis of all Graves's most fundamental preoccupations: his reading in the classics, his conversations with Rivers, his immersion in both Celtic and classical myth and history, and his own firm sense of what was required of a dedicated poet.

Since the Bronze Age, the figure of an all-embracing female deity — a Moon Goddess, an Earth Mother, controlling seasons, fertility, and the cycle of birth and death — had been worshipped throughout Europe until challenged by the male gods of the Graeco-Roman world. With Christianity, goddess worship disappeared, preserved, according to Graves, by poets alone as a divine secret — or through the worship of a muse. From his vast reading, Graves created a monomyth that gave order to his deepest convictions and restored to poetry some of the sanctity he felt it had lost by neglecting myth for reason.

Graves was a deicide; he had made from the great tangle of his existence a religion that he could feel true to, and which could resolve the contradictions and oppositions in his thinking. As a devotee, he was privy to the Goddess's will. He always bowed solemnly nine times at his first sight of the new moon. To the supplanting of the Goddess by a Father God he attributed all the ills of the modern world.

It is, of course, possible to read *The White Goddess* as pure wish fulfilment, as a projection into human history of precisely what Graves needed to believe in, ingeniously disguised as investigative scholarship, which would justify the succession of young, beautiful muses whom Graves lit on in his later years. In it merged his fears and his ecstasies — his exacting mother, his war-horror, his trials with Laura, his sexual terrors and longings, the state of inspiration he equated with being in love, the coming together of dualities in a poem.

At the time, T.S. Eliot worked for Faber & Faber, and although he was somewhat overawed by the manuscript of *The White Goddess*, he was certain of its importance and agreed to publish the book. The war ground to an end, and Graves began to raise his hopes of returning to Spain. He and Beryl now had three children, William, Lucia, and Juan; a fourth, Tomas, was born later, in Deyá. In 1946, Graves pulled strings and received permission to return. In the spring of 1946, a small plane landed them in Palma — Graves, Beryl, and the children. They found that Robert's house, Canelluñ, and its garden had been tended and maintained, books and papers in place. The villagers were delighted at the return of Don Roberto, as an omen of sorts. He had come back, to begin Deyá again.

*

A mountain chain runs along that coast of Majorca, and from its lower slopes the land falls away steeply to the Mediterranean. The coastline is broken by protruding rocky headlands, enclosing long, fertile valleys and small, secret beaches. Deyá comes as a surprise, perched halfway between mountain and sea. The upper part of the village is cone-shaped, with the houses on each other's shoulders, winding down from the church at the crest. Nothing is flat except for the terraces that descend like a series of steps from the base of the overhanging mountain, the Teix, which dominates and dwarfs the village, making it feel small. The terraces are planted with olive trees — puffs of silver-green — and with gnarled almond trees. At sunset, the great wall of the

Teix goes through a constant shifting of colour and shadow: light gold, ochre, amber, deep grey, dark. A short main street is lined with the village's essential outposts — butcher, baker, grocer, telegraphist, garage, café. The folds in the landscape form acoustical traps, so that miscellaneous sounds — the crack of an axe, a mule braying, conversation, the thud of a boat's motor, a girl somewhere singing — float in, breaking the mesmerizing silence. In the hot summer sun, the village seems suspended, half asleep. The land is so up-and-down that every window frames a different view, the air so clear that around the full moon the whole face of the Teix is drenched in bright silver, towering above the sleeping houses, the moonlight almost bright enough to read by.

Spain in the early fifties seemed to be still waking up, coming back to life, docile under Franco. Its frontiers had been sealed off from the rest of Europe since the beginning of the Spanish Civil War, in 1936, and had remained so throughout the Second World War. The country felt worn out, threadbare. Travelling was unpredictable, traffic sparse, food hardly plentiful. Agricultural communities like Deyá, however, had fared better through these lean years, for they could feed themselves, working the land by hand and mule. To local people, shuttered up for so long, foreigners were something of a novelty — a situation that in ten years changed beyond anyone's imagining. Deyá's population in the fifties must have been about five hundred. For the villagers, the foreigners' antics fulfilled the function that television does today.

One evening in the summer of 1953, I was sitting on the terrace of a small *pensión* in Deyá, watching the sunset play itself out on the face of the Teix. I had gone there, with quiet in mind, on the advice of a travel agent — I had no idea that Graves lived there. Suddenly, through the beaded fly-curtain, Robert erupted. He cut a formidable figure — tall, bearlike, with a large torso and head, a straw hat, a straw basket shouldered, and a look set on the edge of truculence. He sat himself down and started asking me a series of questions, as though mapping me. Then he reached for the book I was reading — Samuel Butler's *Notebooks*. He crowed with pleasure and began looking for his favourite passages, telling Butler anecdotes with zest. Abruptly he got up, thanked me for the conversation, and left. After I came to know Robert well, I found that he often assessed people suddenly by some sign — a mannerism, a stray remark, a misplaced enthusiasm. I imagine that if I had been reading Ezra Pound's *Cantos* my memory of Graves might fill no more than this paragraph.

At the time, I was teaching at Sarah Lawrence, which left me long free summers. I had published some poems in *The New Yorker* and also a book of poems, slim in every respect, but I had begun to feel that writing and teaching went uneasily together; I had no idea how to live as a writer, though. What I wanted, emphatically, was to own my own time. It was this that drew me to Robert's existence — how he was able to live in the slow rhythms of Deyá and yet keep up a vigorous writing life. Robert was fifty-eight at the time, a veteran; I was twenty-seven, and an aspirant, no more. It was his lived example that led me to cut loose, to decide to live by writing.

I ran into Robert at odd moments during that summer — at the beach, in the café for the mail delivery, in the village store — and each time he would launch straight into conversation: what he had been writing that day, how to cope with ants. One afternoon, he took me back with him to Canelluñ, his house beyond the village. There, sitting in his workroom, narrow, high-ceilinged, and walled with his essential books, we talked about poetry. At that time, I was immersed in poetry, and read it voraciously; I also knew a whole host of poems by heart. Robert's prodigious memory was even more crammed, and this meant that sometimes, on a walk, one of us would produce a poem from the air which we would then explore with a fine editorial point, questioning it, sometimes rewriting it, or even parodying it. It was a conversational mode we often returned to, as a kind of game.

A few foreigners lived in Deyá the year round — a sculptor, a clutch of painters, a writer or two — for houses were easily available and cheap to rent. It had regular visitors, who returned faithfully each summer, and a few families from Palma summered there with their children. Life was frugal, somewhat bare-boned — water drawn from the well, cooking done on charcoal, electricity supplied by a local turbine that came on at dark and ran until eleven-thirty, when it winked three times and, ten minutes later, candles lit, went out. So simplified, the days seemed slowed. Robert and I exchanged letters over the winter, I returned the following summer, and eventually I resigned from Sarah Lawrence and moved to Spain.

From 1953 on, I spent part of each year in Deyá, usually renting a different village house, whitewashed, sparsely furnished, stony, and cool. I came to know the Graves household very well. Its centre of concern was always Robert, but Beryl, who knew his changes better than anyone else, kept him attached to daily realities — the garden's needs, who was coming when — and she had a way of bringing him back to earth with an oblique humour, which the children caught and copied: they would tease Robert by asking improbable questions, and he would answer in kind, teasing them back.

Robert's children knew his moods well. In quick succession, he could be stern and mischief-bent, angry and benevolent, greedy and fastidious, arrogant and gentle. He was also an inveterate maker of rules, and would blurt them out defiantly at table. He usually forgot them at once, as did his children. I always thought that it was Robert who first pronounced the rule that 'poets shouldn't drive', for he said it to me often enough. When I reminded him of a poet he liked who had once driven a school bus for a living, he only smiled wryly.

Canelluñ sat in a considerable garden, which had to be watered morning and night, and secured against sheep that might stray in. The house looked out to sea, and from a wide hall it gave onto the living room and kitchen on one side and Robert's workroom on the other. I grew used to having him suddenly rise, unplug himself from the conversation, and cross the hall. He would sit at his worktable, dip a steel-nibbed pen into an inkwell, and go on from where he had left off, without forethought or hesitation. When he reached a stopping point, he might wander into the garden, taking his thinking with him; pass through the kitchen absent-mindedly; and return to the text. Quite soon, I realized that, apart from days of emergency or obligation, he wrote every day of his life, not on any strict schedule but whenever a piece of time opened to him. When he wrote, he was detaching himself, composing himself, putting himself in order.

Graves kept away from machinery of any description; I never saw him touch a typewriter. In the thirties, he and Riding had come across a young German Jew whom they immediately took to. They taught him English, then offered him a job as secretary. He left Majorca with them, served in the Royal Navy in the Second World War, and afterward returned, with his family, to work again for Graves, living in a cottage by the entrance to the Canellun garden. His name was Karl Goldschmidt, but he had changed it in the Navy to Kenneth Gay. He had become, through many books, Graves's conscience: he was a meticulous copy-reader. Where Robert's time was concerned, he acted as watchdog, suspicious of strangers. After a morning's work,

Robert would leave his handwritten pages for Karl, and they would be on his desk, immaculately typed, by late afternoon. He would then subject the text to another severe mauling. Eventually, the finished manuscript would be given to Castor, the mailman, when he came to work in the Canelluñ garden. To Robert, the mails were sacred. His mail would be left for him in the village café, and he would appear religiously at the same hour, open his letters, and, very often, share their contents with any friend who was there. He was also a prodigious letter writer, it was nothing for him to fill his inkwell and write some thirty letters in a day — to friends, to editors, to critics, to newspapers. He wrote me once, 'Find a place where things are done by hand, and the mails are trustworthy.' It may have been as well that he antedated the fax machine.

*

Deyá often seemed to me like the stage of an enormous natural amphitheatre, demanding from its new settlers some sacrifice, some drastic behaviour — and, indeed, many dramas took place among those who alighted there, in some of which Robert played a part, inevitably, for he considered Deyá *his* village. It is the setting of many of his poems; it served as his vocabulary — the landscape his thought moved in. He approached new arrivals with curiosity and diffidence. If he took to someone, he would often create, out of a few essential facts, a whole identity, holding it out to the newcomer as though it were a coat that had only to be slipped on to fit. Those who proved unwilling to have their essential selves thus reconstructed would have 'let him down', and the coat would not be proffered again. These identities were fictions of his, fashioned to accommodate strangers into his orbit. In Deyá, he was an insistent Prospero.

During the fifties, the demands of school fees and other expenses kept Robert at his worktable. Late in 1954, he found that he had taken on more work than he could cope with, and he asked me if I would help him by doing a rough first translation of Suetonius's *The Twelve Caesars*, for Penguin, while he himself translated Lucan's *Pharsalia*. I went to work, and every so often Robert would appear, to talk and to check my progress. Ignoring the Latin, he would go over my latest pages, glasses cocked, pencil at the ready, humphing from time to time, leaving behind him an undergrowth of correction. I had done what I considered a finished version, so when he had gone I would pore over his corrections, for they were all improvements. Over that winter, I learned about writing English prose. The severity with which he corrected his own work he would apply equally to the writing of others — a habit that made him an impatient reader of his contemporaries. He became for me then the reader over my shoulder.

I also learned about the mysterious alchemy of translation. Robert was a first-rate classicist, and in the course of writing the two Claudius novels he had immersed himself in Roman history, but, much more than that, he would talk about life in Rome in the first century AD as easily as he would about life in, say, present-day London. In a sense, he had been there.

He decided that Suetonius was part gossip columnist, part obituarist, and had to be rendered in an appropriate English. Sometimes he took questionable liberties with an original text, as he did in his version of the *Iliad*. He could not always keep a rein on his impulse to improve and tidy up a text, even if it was not originally his. The one translation of his that he made into a true English masterpiece, however, is his version of Lucius Apuleius's *The Golden Ass*. It was a text he deeply loved, and he so put on the original the spare clarity and cadence of his own prose that *The Golden Ass* more properly belongs among his own books — he made free with the text, for the sake of its English coherence. A good translator, he insisted, must have *nerve*. Nerve he had, in abundance. I had no idea then that I would turn to translation later in my life, but when I did I began to appreciate that brief apprenticeship, that gift of nerve.

*

Deyá remained quiet throughout the fifties, except for surges of summer visitors. Between books, Robert accepted invitations to write on a variety of subjects, and he took great pride in the swiftness and sureness with which he dispatched these tasks. Writing prose was a precise craft, he maintained, and a writer should be able to give matter of any kind the language it asked for. Robert also left his books behind him, quite literally. In 1956, he undertook to write a novel around the trial of Dr William Palmer, a likable Victorian racegoer and rogue, on a charge of poisoning, for which he was hanged — unjustly, Graves thought. He brought from London all the books he would need as background to the period and set to work. It was as though William Palmer had come to stay in Canelluñ, in Robert's workroom, for Palmer usurped his conversation whenever he emerged. Robert worked on the book strenuously over a two-month period, and when it was finished, immaculately typed by Karl, the books were posted back to his London bookdealer, and William Palmer was never mentioned again.

Poetry, however, was an altogether different matter. Whenever he felt the nudge of a poem, he would put aside all else to make way for it. For him, poems were not just sudden pieces of writing: they were events. He subjected his poems to the same fierce scrutiny to which Laura had subjected them. He had a remarkable ear for the movement of a poem; even his lesser poems are beautifully fashioned. He went through many poetic manners, and was adept in all of them, but latterly he took to suppressing in each new edition of his *Collected Poems* his earlier, crankier poems, in favour of his later muse-poems. Muse-poems were either poems he felt had come to him magically, written from inspiration rather than intent, or poems addressed to a muse —

love poems, but love poems that recast love conflicts in the language and manner of myth, and in which the lovers themselves act out mythical patterns.

Madness and fear of madness loom often in his poems, at the opposite pole from his sturdy common sense. Yet the poems he considered inspired rather than contrived came from the beauty and terror of madness, of the irrational; some of his images he claimed he fully understood only years after writing them. The onset of such madness was what he always feared and longed for: it moved between dream and nightmare, between desire and revulsion: and it came infallibly from falling in love. In writing, however, common sense often had the last word:

> For human nature, honest human nature
> Knows its own miracle: not to go mad.

At that point, into his sixties, Graves occupied a singular and increasingly admired ground among his contemporaries. He had redefined the obligations of the poet, which he sustained by a body of mythological connection, a whole cosmography, and a poetic creed that was coherent and rooted in the past. Few other poets had fulfilled the poet's function with such grave dedication or had cast it in such a visionary light. Only Yeats, whom Graves chose to despise, had sustained poetry with a mythology of his own devising, though one far less well informed and thorough than Graves's.

In workaday Deyá, I saw much of Robert, quite

often with the children and Beryl, on Sunday picnics to the beach, and sometimes alone, in his workroom or at the café. I would question him about the past, about writers like Hardy, whom he had met, whom he could even imitate. He would try out on me the arguments in his current writing, inviting criticism and disagreement, which he usually resisted stoutly, sometimes crossly. He was tigerish over matters of language: his dictionaries were thumbed and ink-stained. He could be infuriating, in his pigheadedness, his often wild misjudgments. His utter disregard for privacy caused trouble between us more than once: he would broadcast matter from close conversations, sometimes recklessly. Robert and I were, however, used to each other. It was difficult to register disagreement with Robert; he was used to sweeping people along with him. With close friends, he would concede differences of opinion, although he clearly viewed them as temporary aberrations. I was often an aberrant friend. In those years, he was writing steadily, even jauntily, enjoying in Deyá a kind of equilibrium that seemed as if it might go on and on, like the agrarian round.

Every so often, word came his way that would give rise to what Beryl always referred to as 'golden dreams'. These stemmed from the time when Alexander Korda contracted to film *I, Claudius*, in 1934, with Charles Laughton as Claudius. Bad luck dogged the film, and it was never finished; but Graves lived from then on in hope of another such windfall. What did come was an invitation in 1956 to lecture in the United States.

Graves had waved off such offers before, but money was now an important consideration, and we held a summit meeting, Robert, Beryl, and I, to talk it over. I had an apartment in New York which he could use as a base, and I promised Beryl that I would travel with him. The arrangements were made, and he set to work preparing three lectures. I went to New York ahead of him, and met him at Idlewild. He arrived somewhat warily; but, startled by the crowds that attended his first lecture, by the discovery that he had unsuspected legions of readers, he expanded, and decided to enjoy himself. Dealing with publishers and editors by mail, Graves generally struck his boxer stance. Meeting them at dinners in his honour, however, he turned benign, and answered questions with his oblique, teasing humour. He visited the *New Yorker* offices and agreed to write stories as well as poems for the magazine. At the Poetry Center of the YMHA, he lectured on *The White Goddess* — by far the most lucid summation he ever made of that 'mad book', as he used to refer to it. He looked the very icon of a poet: magnificent head, crowned with grey curls; stoutly in his own skin; in full command of his flights of argument. In the introduction to one lecture, he explained that on his last visit to America he had lost twenty pounds in weight and two thousand dollars, and that now, having regained the weight, he had come to make good his other loss. He teased his audiences with erudition; they went away spellbound, and bought his books. His visit made it clear to him that he need not worry about money, about the children's school fees: a number of his previous books were to appear in new editions; he had firm commitments for those in the works or in his sights; and there was enough talk of screenplays and movie rights to revive his 'golden dreams'. I had never seen Robert in front of an audience — it seemed to me that he thought only of readers, not of listeners — and was astonished, not just by his utter domination of his listeners but by his extraordinary lucidity. He sounded remarkably sane, but when he read his poems I realized that his mad self was merely lying in wait somewhere for him, and that he expected it and needed it.

Travelling, we replayed his lectures, sorting out the people he had met, paging through books he had been given, bountifully inscribed, and we continued to talk about poetry. Once, on the train from Boston to New Haven, he nudged me. About three rows away was a book face down on the arm of a seat, its owner asleep. It was *The Reader Over Your Shoulder*. I had heard him tell, many times, a possibly apocryphal story about Arnold Bennett, who had carried in his wallet a five-pound note to give to the first person he found reading one of his books: on his death, the note was found, still folded, in his wallet. Graves waited until his reader awoke, and then he moved to an adjoining seat, introduced himself, told his Arnold Bennett story, signed the book, and gave his startled reader ten dollars, swearing he would claim it from his publisher.

We took long walks, in the Village, on the West Side piers. One night, he wanted to see the moon, which we found only after walking a few blocks; at that moment, Deyá was on his mind. Once, in the West Village, he stopped me and pointed: out of a sixth-floor window a horse's head was protruding. The building housed a police livery stable. One evening, returning home, he stopped, silent. After a while he said, gruffly, 'Don't much like that chap.' 'That chap' was Robert himself, at his previous night's lecture. He flew back to Europe, Beryl's shopping list ticked and executed, on a Pan American plane that carried Toscanini's coffin in the back of the cabin. He wrote me a letter from the plane, which arrived in an envelope bearing the legend 'Fly with the stars the Pan American way.' Robert had crossed out 'stars' and written above it 'dead'.

That first trip was something of a coming out for Robert. Where he had previously been reluctant to leave Deyá except for obligatory holidays in England, he now accepted invitations to travel, to give lectures and readings, to write magazine articles, to be featured in a *Playboy* interview. On his travels, he made new friends, some of them in movie circles; Alec Guinness and Ava Gardner both visited him in Deyá. Later, in the sixties, he became something of a cult figure: *The White Goddess* was a source book for readers of *The Whole Earth Catalog*. The BBC came to Deyá to make a television film about him. The State University of New York at Buffalo was preparing to pay him handsomely for the scratched manuscripts he had saved in the attic of Canelluñ. His mail had become voluminous.

As I think of it, that first foray made Robert suddenly

aware that he had not only a literary reputation but a public self — he could enthral an intelligent audience by his wit, the easy way he displayed his great learning, his humour, his downrightness, his poetic intensity, and, of course, the elegance of his language. Clusters of people, many of them young, waited after his lectures to ask him questions or murmur some fervent homage to him. He had more than enough money, and could count on a handsome advance for any new book. He met celebrities who wanted to meet him, and, talking with students, he breathed in some of the early fervour of the sixties. His letters, which were usually full of the family, the garden, and the work in hand, now talked of famous visitors, movie options. His royalties could now make Canelluñ more comfortable, and buy Beryl a new Land Rover. Yet, on that first visit, he had been perfectly conscious that he was playing himself, reinforcing his eccentric image. I think that as he began to travel more he steadily lost that consciousness. Never exactly modest, he became increasingly arrogant, increasingly defiant in his views. The golden dreams, he was certain now, were real.

Change was coming precipitously to Spain at the same time, even to villages as far-flung as Deyá. Mass tourism changed the face of Spain, and was to sustain the Spanish economy into the eighties. Bottled gas replaced charcoal in the kitchen, cars and buses began to multiply on the roads, foreign newspapers appeared in the kiosks. The equilibrium that the village — and

Robert — had enjoyed throughout the fifties was suddenly over forever.

*

In late 1958, I left Deyá, first to sail the Atlantic with some friends in a Nova Scotia schooner, then to remarry and settle in Madrid. I saw much less of Robert after that, but we still exchanged letters. Since I first came across Spain, I had become immersed in it, quite apart from Robert, for Robert's interest in Spain was distant; only his locality, Deyá, concerned him. I learned Spanish through those years, and I travelled all over Spain, looking and listening and reading. In 1960, *The New Yorker* published the first of a series of chronicles I wrote from Spain — anti-Franco, as were all but a few of the Spaniards I knew. Robert scolded me for writing it: it was impolite, he maintained, to criticize one's host. I found this attitude ridiculous, and said so. We stopped short of a serious falling out, but I came to realize that, inevitably, I was withdrawing from Robert's orbit.

Robert had always been ready to laugh at himself; now I felt he was losing his irony. He had grown deeply serious about the Goddess, and, more and more, he laid down her law. I had always viewed the Goddess as a vast, embracing metaphor, and I thought Robert did, too, somewhere in his mind. I never believed in the Goddess, any more than I believed in a Christian God. I realized, however, that Robert did believe, insistently so, and that the belief sustained and justified him.

In late 1959, Robert underwent a prostate operation, in London, which had serious complications. He was found to have a rare blood condition and had to be given massive transfusions, which left him weak for months. To a number of people, his son William included, that trauma had much to do with increasingly irrational behaviour on his part throughout the sixties. The allowances his friends made for him were exceeded by his growing insistence that he was somehow a spokesman for his times, that his long-held views were becoming generally accepted as the truth. It seemed to me when I met him later that year that he was losing all sense of the 'otherness' of other people: now they had only to fit into his script.

*

In *The White Goddess*, addressing the question of why so few poets continued to write throughout their life, Graves explains:

> The reason is that something dies in the poet. Perhaps he has compromised his poetic integrity by valuing some range of experience or other — literary, religious, philosophical, dramatic, political or social — above the poetic. But perhaps also he has lost his sense of the White Goddess: the woman he took to be a Muse, or who was a

Muse, turns into a domestic woman and would have him turn similarly into a domesticated man. Loyalty prevents him from parting company with her, especially if she is the mother of his children and is proud to be reckoned a good housewife; and as the Muse fades out, so does the poet . . . The White Goddess is anti-domestic; she is the perpetual 'other woman', and her part is difficult indeed for a woman of sensibility to play for more than a few years, because the temptation to commit suicide in simple domesticity lurks in every maenad's and muse's heart.

In 1961, he began a poem, 'Ruby and Amethyst', thus:

> Two women: one as good as bread,
> Bound to a sturdy husband.
> Two women: one as rare as myrrh,
> Bound only to herself.

In July of 1960, I went to visit him in Deyá briefly, for his birthday, with my wife and son. Robert as a baby had been touched on the head by Swinburne while being wheeled in his pram on Wimbledon Common; I had Robert touch Jasper on the head, for continuity's sake. Robert was newly consumed by a letter from the agent William Morris, who had suggested that *The White Goddess* might make a singular film, and he had been asked to provide an outline, for which he had made notes. Would I take them and see what I could make of them? The notes were indeed fertile, even daring in places. Then he wrote me, once I was back in Madrid, that he had found the person who must play the White Goddess. He had also found a new muse.

She was Canadian by nationality, with a Greek father and an Irish mother, and she was called Margot Callas. Graves met her in Deyá during that summer of 1960, and was instantly entranced by her. She was intelligent, witty, highly intuitive, certainly beautiful, and it was not long before Robert was discovering a clutch of other qualities in her. It was not long, either, before new poems began to flow from him, and Margot occupied his whole mind. Once more, the Goddess had sent him a sign.

Not for the first time, or the last, Graves was captivated by what he pronounced firmly to be a manifestation of the Goddess. On each occasion, he became possessed, partly mad; on each occasion, he wrote, furiously, poems, only poems. He would shower his muse with them, and with letters and tokens of faith. Beryl, who knew him best, accepted these muses with a calm that others found inexplicable: she had learned how necessary they were to him. As in his years with Laura, he would refuse to hear a word against his muse. Now, as high priest, as voice, he spoke for the Goddess: only he could interpret her wishes, her commands.

Toward the end of 1960, I had to go to New York briefly, and I went by way of London, where the Graves family had gone for a Christmas visit. Robert spoke only of Margot, obsessively, and gave me some letters and tokens to take to her in New York. I did not know then what that would mean.

I remember that snow was lying in the city when I arrived, and that I went first thing to *The New Yorker*, to turn in a piece. I spent ten days busily, made plans to sail back to Spain on the Leonardo da Vinci, and delivered Robert's tokens to Margot. She, too, was returning to Spain, and took a cabin on the same ship.

Inevitably, we talked during the voyage about Robert. She, too, was taken aback by the insistence in his redefinition of her. She had been given no say in the matter; in Robert's eyes, her muse status required only her acquiescence, and her nature was anything but acquiescent. We talked of many things besides Robert, and during the voyage realities intervened: Margot and I fell precipitously in love. By the time we reached Spain, we were lost in each other, and had decided to leave behind our present lives. She made her way to Majorca, I to Madrid. A month later, we met up in France, and came to rest in a water mill in the French Basque country. Robert was not on my mind.

I had not thought what his reaction might be, but I could not have imagined its ferocity. Margot came in for no criticism: the Goddess had swung her axe, as predicted. I came in for all his rage. She was no longer muse, I no longer poet. The poems that followed our desertion claimed the next section of the *Collected*

Poems. It was not until later that I saw this as a pattern that had arisen several times before. In the mythic pattern of *The White Goddess* the poet succumbs to the rival as the inevitable death-in-love that he must undergo; in reality, however, the rival became the arch-betrayer. Robert, in those slowly declining years, came to see his reality wholly in terms of mythic inevitability; and the myth was his alone.

We never spoke again, Robert and I. Over the years, Margot and I had many meetings and partings. I would hear of Robert occasionally, for I still saw friends we had in common. New settlers had flocked to Deyá, and land was being snapped up, houses were being built. It had grown too busy to be any longer Robert's village. The Goddess proved ever more insistent: a new muse had manifested herself, and Robert was once more writing poems — muse-poems.

When his *Complete Poems* are published, I think they will reveal that in his strongest poems Robert is less a love poet than a poet of opposition and contradiction, of two-mindedness, much more questioner than worshipper. His muse-poems, finely wrought and tense as they are, all follow the same single-minded plot. Some read like imitations of him — perhaps because the muses he chose latterly were more and more his own creations. The stance he struck became ever more adamant, even shrill. I think he had stopped listening — to those close to him, to his own common-sense self, even to his own misgivings.

Of the thousand-odd poems that Robert wrote, I can

think of a considerable handful that are sufficiently strong and singular as to belong unquestionably to the canon of English poetry. That may seem meagre; but what most distinguishes him as a poet, I think, is how he chose to live, his dedication to the office of poet. In the first chapter of *The White Goddess* he wrote:

> Since the age of fifteen poetry has been my ruling passion and I have never intentionally undertaken any task or formed any relationship that seemed inconsistent with poetic principles; which has sometimes won me the reputation of an eccentric.

That remained his measure, all his long life.

Robert's vindictiveness toward me did not reach me except by rumour, and there I was hurt mostly by its untruths. I felt for Beryl, but she was wisest in Robert's ways, and, giving him the room he needed, she allowed him his follies, whether wishful or actual. I had my own work to do, and I continued to do it, just as Robert would have. I realized then, as I do now, that many of my writing habits I absorbed from him, like the sanctity of the writing table, which I set up wherever I am. I remain attached to village life and to the agricultural round. When Margot and I first parted, I bought a small house on the edge of a Spanish mountain village, and spent every summer there with my son Jasper. For the last ten years, I have gone every winter to the Dominican Republic, where I have a house above the sea, and where, honed to essentials, the days simplify and slow down, as they did in Deyá. I revise what I write, scrupulously. I still bow nine times to the new moon; and I still read his poems, or listen to them in my head.

In the spring of 1985, I made a brief visit to Spain, with Margot, to visit Deyá, to see Beryl and some of the children, and to take farewell of Robert. His mind and memory had been failing steadily, and now he lay on a cot in the room adjoining his workroom, dozing, silent, beyond communication. It was as though he had gone into one of his trances and had not returned from it. At one moment, however, his eyes opened and widened; and it seemed to me that in them still lay all the wisdom and mischief in the world.

From 'Notes from a Spanish Village'

You cannot stumble on the village. For one thing, the road ends there, and, for another, you cannot see it from below — not until the church looms above you, and houses begin to show on the carefully groomed terraces, dotted haphazardly here and there, with no apparent access. Around the last, climbing corner, more of the village appears, as though the houses had suddenly shown themselves in order to see who was coming. It is a perplexing place, in that it has no real centre except a quiet paved square beside the church. It has grown up among the terraces that line two bowls in the steep side of the valley. Each house appears to have been conceived separately. There are no streets. The paved road becomes a dust road, then a track winding up and up. Above the top rim, the sky is fiercely blue. My son and I have often tried to make a map of the place, but it defeats us; only an aerial photograph would show the curious contours of the ground. We are used to being surprised by the place — by the way each house looks out on a different village, a different-shaped mountain. The mountains set the atmosphere — grey rocky crests hazy in the heat, with a fringe of pines on the tree line and, on the lower slopes, olive groves and long rows of darker-green almond trees. We climb steadily up, with the slow, bent-kneed plod that the villagers use, turning to look down over the village, a patchwork of ochre roofs and green terraces, and then we walk over the crest onto a small, fertile plateau, on the far corner of which stand our house and, beside it, a little ilex forest, which falls steeply away to the next valley, far below. From the house, there is no trace of the village, and no sound other than the jangle of goat bells, or the bark of the dog on the adjoining farm. Sitting on the stone terrace, I can hear insects rustling in the wheat, the whirr of birds' wings, the stirring of leaves. Sounds of our well — the rattling chain, the thud and plunge of the bucket, the creak of the wheel — loom loud in the attention. Over the village hangs the same towering silence. The hollows form acoustical traps, so conversations across the valley will float into hearing, the words just indistinguishable but the tune clear. The sound of an occasional car does not break the silence so much as puncture it slightly, thus underlining it. On still afternoons, we can hear the children singing in the forest, shepherded by the nuns. The silence is such that we are careful about breaking it.

*

I first went to Spain in the early fifties, almost by accident — certainly without forethought, for I knew and felt little about the country beyond a strong antipathy for the Franco regime. I had not been there very long, however, before it dawned on me that Spain was going to matter a great deal to me, and become a part of my life; I found it recognizable at once, in the way that something one has been looking for subconsciously is recognizable. What caught me so quickly was an energetic sense of immediacy, a relish for the living moment: when Spaniards sat down at a table, they instinctively shed any preoccupation other than that with the food in front of them and with the immediate company. Their past was too brutal to bear remembering, their future out of their hands, so they chose to live in a vivid, existential present, which made conversation easy and open in spite of the pervasiveness of the regime. At that time, too, they were delighted by the appearance of foreigners among them, being curious, hungry for some notion of a way of life other than their own, because they had been cut off from other countries from 1936 until 1948 and longed for anything to break the stalemate of their isolation. The shame of the Civil War still hung over everything, a brutal ghost, from whose shadow the people were tentatively emerging. Doubts remained, however, and the few scattered foreigners who showed up provided some hope, some positive distraction. The country was poor and without luxury of any kind, but a simple dignity abounded, a graceful rhythm that soon had me converted. I set out to learn and explore as much of Spain as I could — the language, the terrain, the history, the character. To enter another culture from choice is always invigorating: we do not have any habits, so everything catches the attention and becomes grist to our minds. Not to know the word for, say, soap can be exasperating, but learning it is a small adventure in which the soap glows momentarily, as though seen for the first time. Even street names start up trails of discovery. Who was General Goded? Finding out unravels the whole complex knitting of the Civil War. We discover a new past, wholly different from our own.

*

Communications in the village depend on word of mouth, and are at the mercy of memory. In the store, Doña Anna tells me that Don Anselmo wishes to see me, though she cannot remember when she got the message. At my convenience, she says. But I walk down the spiralling path right away, respectful of the summons. Don Anselmo occupies an extraordinary position in the village — virtually that of headman. Although he has given up being mayor after almost forty years, he is deferred to and consulted regularly, and everywhere he is shown the same reverent respect. Stories about him abound, for from time immemorial he has been called in to arbitrate every kind of dispute, quarrel, or disagreement in the village and its surrounds, and locally his judgments ring as famously as those of Sancho Panza — even among the foreigners, who have often come to him for counsel. A broad, bulky man, he is profoundly ugly, massively ugly, except that his ugliness is easily trounced by the tangible kindness of his look and manner. He owns and runs a small *pensión*, which has the village's only bar and terrace. He bought it, he told me once, so that those who wanted to see him would always know where to find him. Don Anselmo has never bothered much about the *pensión*, except that he likes to do the cooking, and I often talk to him in the kitchen while he is preparing soup or skinning rabbits. The bar is sparse and bare, with family photographs on the walls and a huge stuffed armchair that serves as Don Anselmo's rostrum. I owe to him almost everything I know about the village; he has both a prodigious memory and a voluminous journal and can reach back not only through his own lifetime but practically to the village's coming into being, for his father was mayor before he was, and he claims the ancestral memory as his own. He is not only well informed but endlessly curious; he questions me often about the foreigners — where they come from, what they do, what they feel about the village. Some of them he likes, others he treats with a grave formality.

On the day I got his message from Doña Anna, I found him deep in his chair, gazing into thought, the newspaper unopened on his lap, his face furrowed like a ploughed field. 'How goes it?' I asked him. 'Well enough,' he replied. 'But my wife has given me all these illustrious articles to read, and it has propelled me to think very much and to wish to consult with you.' He waved at a pile of magazines beside the chair, and, picking them up one after another, I found that they were all opened to articles on automobile pollution. I realized what had been happening. Don Anselmo's wife, a bright, birdlike woman, is a great devourer of magazines and serves as a kind of information bank for her husband. Don Anselmo was wearing his prophetic look. 'I'm thinking of talking with Guillermo about banning cars from the village.' He eyed me speculatively.

'But, Don Anselmo, there are hardly twenty cars in the place!'

'Twenty-two,' he corrected me. 'And I realize that they affect neither our air nor our chests in any serious way. The only nuisance they do is to come back late and wake up Nicolás in the house by the road. He is old and needs his sleep. No, it is only that I have been reading these learned articles, and I am astonished that in the face of this terrible knowledge not a single town has taken any step to confront the matter. For that reason, I am of the opinion that we must take the step, although we are not in immediate danger. It might lead other places to follow our example. First, I thought I would consult with you over what the foreigners might think. Would they understand? They must certainly be more conscious of this pollution than we are. I intend to talk to them, in any case.'

Don Anselmo's plan never quite came to pass, although it preoccupied the village for some time. Were the number of cars to increase, Guillermo announced, they would all have to be left on the level ground below the church. But it is an unlikely prospect. Next year, in accordance with Spanish educational policy, the village school will be closed down and the children taken by bus to a central regional school some thirty kilometres away, in the market town. Those families with children may very well move closer to the school, closer to civilization; some have already made the decision. Don Anselmo, in despair, proposed a voluntary school in the village, for both foreign and local children. 'We could have the first multilingual village in all Spain,' he announced dramatically, throwing his arms wide. I wish that every one of his plans had come into being.

*

Eugenio, who comes to turn over the terraces and cut back the almond trees, tells me the wistful history of the village every year. From its beginnings, the village's main sustenance came from making charcoal and cutting wood to burn, thus fuelling the surrounding countryside. The men would go out from Monday to Friday onto the long wooded slope behind the village, extending halfway up the mountain, to build the careful piles of small wood and twig, which were sealed over except for a small escape at the top. The wood smouldered away, eventually turning into charcoal. For their cooking, the villagers always started the charcoal outside, in a three-legged stove, over a fire of twigs, and then transferred it, red-hot, with tongs, to iron burners set in tile in the kitchen, fanning it with woven-straw fans that the women of the village made in their houses. The women were also very skilful at drying and preserving food for the men to take out with them during the week. The men slept out, and Eugenio showed me a sumptuous sleeping bag he had sewn for himself out of sheepskins, which he never uses now. Around 1958, butane gas in cylindrical containers made its appearance, and in no time *butagas* had transformed the countryside. It was, of course, easier to use than charcoal, but, more than that, it seemed to show that Spain was creeping forward after being stagnant for so long. For the charcoal burners, however, gas meant that their work stopped dead. Most of them were able to find jobs in construction, because the building boom had begun by then; for that, though, they had to leave the village — sometimes for good. It felt as if the place had surrendered all its energy and slumped into disuse. Don Anselmo did his best to animate the place, with schemes to buy looms and to found a pottery, but the villagers had fallen victims to a disheartened listlessness. Besides, by then a handful of foreigners had settled in the place, and work on their houses, or in their houses, kept the village ticking over, in a semiretired kind of way. I still get charcoal from Eugenio, who prepares a pair of burnings every year, but the straw fans have disappeared forever. Don Anselmo remains hopeful. 'I can see a time coming when they will be pleading with us to make charcoal again,' he says. 'Oil and gas will give out, and we shall become an important source, I know it. I have longings to see our village come back to life. That it may still be possible sustains me as I decline.' What Don Anselmo never mentions is that the men of the village supplemented their money from making charcoal by picking up and distributing contraband cigarettes, until the contraband traffic dwindled, roughly when the charcoal did. He refuses to hear any mention of contraband. Even his optimism about charcoal he keeps for public occasions; when he talks in private, I can see how thoroughly he has identified the dying of the village with his own dying.

*

After Franco became head of state, his photographic likeness was displayed prominently in all town halls throughout Spain. Every few years, a new photograph was sent around, so that the Spanish people might be suitably attuned to the growth in stature of their little Generalissimo. As mayor, Don Anselmo received these photographs over the years and duly hung the current likeness in the small office that serves as town hall. He did not, however, destroy the old photographs but kept them carefully. One day, he motioned to me and told me he had something to show me. He led the way along a back corridor, up a few steps, to a locked door, which he opened with a key he produced from his wallet. The room was stale and dusty, entirely empty except for a single straight wooden chair, but around the walls hung, in sequence, a whole row of official photographs of Franco. As my eyes moved slowly along the walls, Franco aged steadily, almost imperceptibly. Don Anselmo put his hand on my shoulder. 'I would appreciate that you do not mention this in the village,' he said solemnly. 'I come here from time to time to meditate on mortality, on the mortality of all of us. I find it curiously comforting. A new picture is due next year, and Guillermo has promised it to me. I have the feeling it may end the series. But I have said that before. Now, let us leave. I feel that at this stage a glass of wine might be appropriate.' He locked the door carefully, but the photographs have remained in my head.

*

Tourism washed over the village, leaving it unperturbed, if not untouched. At one time, busloads of tourists used to labour up the road and spill out into the small square, perhaps lured by the prospect of seeing Spain as it once was, but there was nowhere for them to go and nothing for them to do. As often as not, they would find Don Anselmo asleep in his armchair, the priest asleep on his porch, and a pervasive, yawning indifference to their presence — and to their custom, for Don Anselmo runs his *pensión* as an amplification of his house, without thought of profit. A small handful of foreigners live permanently in the village, but either they have chosen the place for its staunch sense of privacy or they are fiercely eccentric — like the Brigadier, who day after day pores over his campaign maps, waiting for the Second World War to resume. Every now and again, someone from the outside world decides that the village is a private Eden, crying out to be shared with an imported elite. We watch with some alarm as the building begins, the mason and the carpenter pitching in with faintly uncomfortable pleasure over having work to hand. But not all ideas of Eden coincide. Prospective buyers come and go, dithering over their decisions. To some, the silence looks alarmingly like total suspension. Refrigerators and swimming-pool filters, moreover, lie far beyond the technological resources of the village, and more than one foreigner has fled the place in despair, the idyll lost for want of a stop valve. The most threatening settler to date was a Swiss woman who envisioned the village as a setting for her own private arts festival, and who whipped up a cluster of small chalets, with pool and performing space, to house her captive celebrities. She goaded and bullied her workmen to the point where she had hired and fired every available hand in the place, earning herself a staggering collection of unrepeatable nicknames. The artists she managed to lure there left after a few days, discovering that they were expected to serve as lapdogs — that their main function was to relieve the boredom of their patroness. Judging by the gleam I notice in local eyes whenever she is mentioned, I would not be surprised to see her houses begin to crumble in the course of the coming year.

*

To come to rest in the village from somewhere in the outside world is not the easiest of transitions, and those who try it occasionally find themselves the victims of 'village paranoia'. They abuse or assault the mailman, or complain that the phone in the *estanco* is tapped. The victims gradually begin to suffer from their chosen isolation and often conjure up a conspiracy that winds in the whole village, down to its animals and machines. The postman is accused of burning letters or throwing them away, but since he is quite prone to do this, the accusation serves nothing but the paranoia. The villagers treat such an outbreak with uncommon indulgence. They have seen it before and look on it as an unfortunate but inevitable consequence of civilization. But then they are indulgent of any eccentricity, among themselves as well, looking on it as no more than the expression of extreme differentiation. A bald Venezuelan violinist who once lived there, in a solitary house on the crest, had such delusions of social superiority that he insisted that his house be known as the Castle. The villagers not only complied but addressed him in the bar, in the store, in the *estanco*, on the road, as 'Your Excellency'. Sebastián, who drives the bus to town, stops sometimes at a spot where his grandfather went over the edge and gets out to pray. And when Javier, the shepherd, comes down in the afternoon to sit on the wall outside the *pensión* and carries on a long conversation with his dog, those who pass are careful to greet the dog as well as Javier, whether the dog is there or not. I often get the notion that the villagers look on the foreigners among them as a species of household pet, for I have overheard them on the bus comparing the antics of various foreign households, as excited as if the presence of these strange people were a running comedy, an endless television serial. Only drunkenness turns them cold; any willing surrender of dignity reduces them to a tight silence.

*

At one time the only telephone in the village was in the *estanco*, the store that sells tobacco and stamps in a wooden kiosk set back in one corner, surrounded by wine barrels and sacks of beans. Consuelo, who runs the store, came in from her kitchen drying her hands, put on her spectacles wearily, and cranked the apparatus before asking for a number in Frankfurt or New York, while the caller fidgeted on the sacks. Most of the foreigners have learned the inside of that store by heart at some time or other, because a call either came through with disturbing speed or took the best part of two days. Waiting does different things to callers: some of them rushed from the store in rage or tears; others fell asleep or drank themselves into silence; and one Dutch girl, under Consuelo's tuition, learned the Spanish word for every object in the place. In private, Consuelo complains bitterly about the telephone, for she has to suffer a bleak series of uncomprehending and incomprehensible rages. One year, she was so beset by foreign hysteria in the *estanco* that she pleaded with Don Anselmo to have the telephone removed altogether, and he managed to placate her only by praising her forbearance (she is infuriatingly taciturn) and pointing out that without the unfortunate machine no one would be able to summon the doctor, who lives in the next village (another cause of foreigners' hysteria). Myself, I suspect that Consuelo revels in these long delays — not so much because she wants company in the store as because she has that most Spanish distrust of mechanisms and any dependence on mechanisms. Not without justification do the villagers associate the coming of machines with the coming of foreigners, who did bring in a whole host of pumps, generators, filters, sprinklers, tractors, and assorted vehicles, without which the village had existed quite happily, and all of which made noise. (Spaniards, of course, want all of them or want none of them.) Julián, the nearest we have to a mechanic, does his job with brilliant eccentricity. One day, he fitted an ingenious ratchet stop of his own devising to our well wheel, to take the weight of the bucket; yet he has never made another. He has kept the postman's prewar motorbike running by making spare parts in his shop, but he dislikes new cars and repairs them warily and bizarrely: the Brigadier's car would start only with the glove compartment open after Julián had been at it. 'I like to be boss of the machine, even to make it,' he once told me. 'Machines should be single things. Something is needed? Something is solved. But when the machines all come at me, ready-made and perfect, there is no place for me.' I know what he means. Our house remained for years a place of perfect silence, for although we had electricity, we scarcely used it, following the sun instead. Ultimately, however, I bought a refrigerator, which starts up through the night with a thunderous purr. I am waiting for it to break down, so that I can give it to Julián, in the interests of research.

*

The attraction of Spain in the nineteen-fifties lay in its apparent permanence. It was well out of the technological stream, and it had the kind of climate that simplifies physical existence, besides being cheap to live in. Most of all, it had an immemorial look and feel, the landscape bleached and whittled down, the rhythm stark and clear, the style frugal. (Ironic now to realize that those who settled there became, unwittingly, the impulse behind the destruction of that rhythm — but since the dignified frugality of the Spaniards stemmed from poverty and lack, such retrospections are self-indulgent. Only a minority of Spaniards feel, as Don Anselmo does, the loss of that equilibrium as a tragedy.) People strayed to Spain from mixed motives. It served as a mecca for alcoholics, with liquor cheap and available always, just as it attracted would-be bullfighters and flamenco dancers, moths round that antique lamp. Writers and painters dug themselves in quite happily, since they were looking, above all, for time, and Spain seemed as close as anyone could come to a continuum. Yet living there became something of a test, for the simple life, as anyone who has embarked on it must know, can turn out to be insurmountably complicated in its mechanics, and quite often sends would-be villagers screaming back to civilization. To set up a small, self-contained world, ignoring the surrounding currents, proves too much for all but a few hardened eccentrics. Those who settled in Spain in small, elitist groups suffered the isolation of castaways: the silence drummed on the roof like rain, and news from home became the only reality. A clear distinction has to be made between tourists, expatriates, and foreigners. Tourists descend on a place in obedient droves, like migrant birds, either following well-beaten tracks or creating them for other tourists. For them, to be in a foreign country is a change, a difference, a chosen astonishment. Above all, their stay is, by definition, temporary and pleasure-bent. Spaniards regarded tourists as a badge of well-being and economic health until they began arriving on a seemingly endless belt, forcing the country to feed, fuel, and amuse them at a thoroughly un-Spanish rate. For once, the fatalism of the Spaniards served them badly: their hospitality lost them their house. Expatriates behave quite differently. They have left their own countries on a long lead, never quite severing the link with home, never quite adapting themselves to their exile, clinging to one another for company, haunting post offices, magazine stands, and banks, waiting expectantly for money from home, anything at all from home. Expatriates are generally getting their own countries into perspective, to the point where they feel strong enough, or desperate enough, to return to them. Foreigners, conversely, live where they are, leaving their pasts and countries behind them for the place they take root in. In one sense, they are lucky: they are free to enter a new context unencumbered, with clear eyes, and are often able to savour a place in a way that escapes the inhabitants, for whom it has become habit. But however well a foreigner adapts himself to a place and its inhabitants, however agile he becomes in the lore and language, there is a line he can never cross, a line of belonging. He will always lack a past and a childhood, which are really what is meant by roots.

*

The real frontier to cross is that of the language. The Spaniards themselves are not famous with other languages — not as linguistically accommodating as, say, the Dutch, who can shift languages imperturbably. They do, however, have great linguistic kindness, in that anyone with a minimal supply of Spanish discovers conversations being put together for him, being turned into small language lessons for his benefit. At first, Spanish is an easy language to enter — regular, uncomplicated, straightforward to pronounce — and most foreigners who settle in Spain quickly acquire a form of 'kitchen' Spanish, which allows them to shop, ask directions, go to banks and offices, and order in restaurants. However, that stage may well become a plateau on which they stay, enacting formal conversations, the language technically accurate but without much emotion. Germans probably speak the most wooden Spanish of all, striding through sentences and subduing them one by one, while the English wield it with a mixture of distaste and disbelief, as though not sure it will work. But so kind are Spaniards that their talk will often limp along in sympathy with any stranger making heavy weather. In the village, this comes to be something of a problem; Joaquín, the mason, for instance, has done so much building for newcomers to the language that when he is explaining anything he cannot help breaking into a kind of baby talk, which his workers now all imitate. Don Anselmo's wife is often pressed to give language lessons, but she is so energetic that she has acquired three extra languages over the years while her pupils floundered about in chapter 1 of *Don Quixote*. Not that language is insurmountable. Little Doña Anna, who in her store has to confront shopping lists in Finnish as a matter of course, has evolved a series of elaborate mimes for recipes and foodstuffs, which bring extra-linguistic results — prodigious performances from hungry aliens, who circle balletically round plump Doña Anna, waving arms and drawing animals and vegetables in the air. The greater hazards arise with those who cannot bear to undergo the embarrassment of learning a new language, and pretend to know it or, at least, to subdue it. We have one such eccentric settler, who after some years believed that

Spanish had descended on him by osmosis. Whenever Spanish was directed at him, he would nod vigorously and say, '*Sí, sí, sí!*' It served him well enough until one day Joaquín came to replace a tile on his roof. When the mason had finished, he gesticulated at the roof and made a small emphatic speech in Spanish, to which our neighbour replied with his usual '*Sí, sí, sí!*' A couple of days later, he came back from the town to find his house being completely reroofed and Joaquín and his men beaming at him enthusiastically.

*

In the course of summer, friends come to visit, and once they have got over their first awe of air and silence, tried their hand at drawing water, wielded hoe and spade, made their own solitary forays to Doña Anna's store to bone up on her vast and complex lexicon of gestures (returning on occasion with unlikely purchases but delighted nevertheless with the exchange of extra-linguistic good will), they find their own crowded worlds receding and get used to drowsing away the afternoons in a hammock in the ilex forest, attempting to sketch the asymmetrical bulk of the mountain that looms behind us, reading the books I surely now know by heart, and in general reducing their lives to a rhythm that other modes of civilization have made impossible. Some of them come with a firm intention of mastering Spanish, step by step, hour by hour, but the rhythm of our village is not one that makes for the pursuit of firm intentions, and over the years I have inherited an impressive collection of Spanish grammars. With time, the outside world does subside and diminish, and the visitors fall in with the rhythm of the sun, waking and sleeping in accordance with a natural order, not with their own. It comes more easily to some than to others — than to those, say, who have turned the ringing of the telephone into a natural sound and grow anxious in its absence. To settle down in the village is a conversion of a kind, and although I am practised at it by now, it still takes time, because one is rooted forever in two worlds, and for some people the simplification that village existence requires may be — however desirable — forever impossible.

*

Below the house, thickly overgrown and by now scarcely distinguishable from the undergrowth, stand the walls of seven houses, their roofs long gone. We often walk among the ruins, for they exude silence like a message and give an odd aura to everything — the mountains hazy through the window sockets, the toolmarks on the stone, the rusted iron rings in the walls. The goats eye us indignantly, their bells clanking as they withdraw to the end of their tethers. We have used some of the tumbled stones from the ruins in laying a stone terrace, embedding them in the ground with their flattest surfaces uppermost — a caveman's jigsaw puzzle. We have been given the history of the houses many times. At the turn of the century, they, along with our house and the adjoining farm, formed a separate, self-sustaining *aldea*, a small village of close to two hundred people; indeed, I have seen it marked on survey maps of the time — a round, emphatic dot. The story of its decline is a recurring one in Spain: the young people moved to the larger village below; there were not enough hands to attend to crops and animals and maintenance; the old people were left alone with the children; the place faltered, failed, and was abandoned. The house we occupy would have been one of the ruins by now if we had not shored it up, but, with the ruins below, it is not hard to feel like a castaway or a survivor. Once, I came back to the house after a hiatus of two years to find that the vegetation had marched tall across the terrace and was fingering the front door. I felt I was just in time. Sitting beside the well on an evening of silk dark, with stars crowding the sky, I find it easy to imagine the village without any human presence whatever — all signs soon consumed by inexorable vegetal muscles, the fruit thudding to the ground unheard. We are the most strident and extravagant species on the whole planet, but not the most durable, as the ruins keep saying. The house feels more and more like an outpost; the insects and the plants have designs on it. I hope sooner or later to make peace with them.

*

Through the glass door of the café I catch sight of

Gonzalo, the mailman, and I go in pursuit of him, for he is famously elusive and, I suspect, secretly disapproves of mail. He is not only the mailman but an itinerant gardener, and in the village they will tell you with great mirth how, while he works, he is prone to park a bundle of letters in the fork of a tree, where they will be found years later, wound round with growing ivy. Scratching himself gloomily, he leads me to his office and produces a handful of letters and two telegrams, all long out of date. He is a hoarder of unopened letters, a renowned inducer of paranoia. This time, he is more disgruntled than usual. 'Nine newspapers a day used to come to this village,' he tells me, 'and nobody minded when they got them. Now I have to deliver thirty every day, and magazines besides, and everybody pursues me. Why can't they listen to the radio?' I walk back to the café in the glinting sun and find Don Anselmo in his armchair, newspapers all around him. For years, he has worried about the fate of the village, having seen it dwindle from a healthy, settled community that thrived on agriculture and charcoal-making for fuel (not to mention contraband) to a skeletal place populated mainly by the old, its terraces uncultivated, its trees uncared for, and some of its houses sold to foreigners or to Spaniards from the city. At Christmas, most of these houses are shuttered and dark, their scattered swimming pools filled with green slime. Only a few hardened settlers stay the year round — people who have burned their bridges, painters obsessed with the light, hopeful novelists, refugees from their old lives, waiting for the mail and dreaming of cities. For the local people, they form a captive layer in the village, cared for like communal village pets, nicknamed, talked about. But they adapt in different ways, to different degrees. For some, the village remains a setting into which they fit themselves with all the trappings of their former lives, brushing aside the language and becoming sturdy custodians of their own habits, like the few resolute English, who walk their dogs, fetch their out-of-date newspapers, and have supplies of tea sent out to them. Others adapt with zeal, learning local lore and dialect, to create for themselves what they are missing; namely, a past in the place. I used often to brood on the possibility of living there all the year round, but I decided I could do so only if I were to plunge into the business of working the land and living by an agrarian calendar. Eugenio always encourages me, for he tells me that on most days he finds himself the only person moving in the vast landscape — a mournful experience; but he clearly expects me to turn up with half a dozen able-bodied helpers, for nothing less would rouse the stony terraces from their present sloth. No matter how close we foreigners come to the village and the villagers, however, life there can never take on for us the inevitability it has for them. There is always for us the choice of going somewhere else — a choice they have never entertained.

*

Eugenio's wife, Josefa, was born in the house and has looked after it for years as though it were a shrine, appearing after storms to see if perhaps a tile on the roof has loosened. Lately, she has taken to eking out Eugenio's seasonally variable profits by looking after the empty houses of the more affluent (and consequently more absent) foreigners, and this activity makes her the most difficult person in the place to track down. I recall Easter two years ago, when I went to my house by chance, and had to recover the keys from Josefa. She was on her caretaking rounds, but the first two swimming-pooled houses I called at were most un-Spanishly chained shut. I ran her to ground in the house of an absentee Irish tycoon, and she insisted on settling me in his most expansive armchair, pressing on me his best brandy in a balloon glass and a cigar from his humidor, while she filled me in on village happenings. She is powerfully hospitable, but she prefers the houses in her charge to their owners, absences to presences. She scrutinizes visitors to our house, for she feels that they ought to suit it rather than it them. She always questions me anxiously about the house, afraid I may sell it or somehow transform it. But I can always reassure her, for over the years I have become as possessed by the sturdy quiet of the place as she is. Was I going to make a road for cars to reach the house, since I had the right to, she once asked me. I told her that I had decided instead to build a drawbridge. I think she still wonders when I am going to begin.

*

To stop at Doña Anna's store is an imperative, and its contents are as familiar to me as a working bookshelf — I can reach instinctively for what I need. She emerges from the gloom at the back, a bantam librarian, at any hour of the waking day. Summer, with its abundant custom, lends her benevolence; in winter she is testier, knitting away the time. We have reached an arrangement over the years whereby she tots up my purchases on strips of newspaper, saving them in a drawer until just before I leave, when she sets aside an evening to add them all up, again and again, touching her thumb to her fingers. A pocket calculator would change her life, in every sense; but the luxury of not carrying money is worth the stumbling of her fingers and thumb, however much it may cost me — or her.

*

Although I know only a few of the foreigners who live in the place — there are supposed to be twenty-seven, but no one seems in a position to make an accurate count, since one or two have apparently not been seen for years — I know the nicknames of a good many of them. The villagers never attempt to pronounce foreign names but have a collective genius for fastening identifying nicknames to the strangers in their midst — and, indeed, they do it to one another, too. The nicknames have a knack of settling on the most distinguishing characteristics: a Dutchman who remains here to nurse his alcoholism is known as Señor Sacacorchos, Mr Corkscrew, and actually has a corkscrew look; a finicky Englishman with the habit of checking all his pencilled bills for errors is called El Matemático, the Mathematician; a German who is wont to talk to imaginary animals is known as El Ventrilocuo; a Venezuelan violinist and his blonde, parrot-tempered wife are always referred to together as Los Demoledores, the Wreckers, so often does the sound of breaking glass and furniture resound from their enraged house. But who is the one they call La Sudadora, She Who Sweats? And will I be able to recognize La Manoteadora, She Who Waves Her Hands, in a place where everyone does? I'm sure I will. Not many know their own nicknames, for the system is so arranged as to give the impression to everyone that he is the nicknameless exception. I know mine through the accident of coming down behind Gonzalo's house one afternoon while he was trying to identify the recipient of an overseas letter as his wife ran through the whole cast of nicknames before my ears. But, for luck's sake, I would no more reveal it than I would leave nail clippings or hair trimmings lying about.

*

One day, the sound of the bell floats up from the church. We stop talking. It goes on tolling. We stand still and listen to it. In a small place of around a hundred souls, which is what we number in summer, a death reverberates. Who has died? Antonio, the retired baker, who reads only old newspapers and so is always full of strange news? Consuelo, who used to sell us chickens, all of which she knew by name? The old people inhabit a continuum in the village. They are its most permanent fixtures, they are honoured and listened to, and their absence remains tangible. When we go down later in the day, people are standing about in twos and threes, talking. Consuelo, on her terrace, is wearing a black shawl. It is Doña Esperanza, of the high orchard, who has died, after being ill for more than a year. I remember her as someone wrapped in sadness. Doña Anna has closed her store. The whole village has stopped. Joaquín the mason, Doña Esperanza's nephew, is sitting on the wall outside the café, strange and grave in suit and tie. Inside, Don Anselmo silently hands a glass of brandy to everyone who enters. There is not much conversation. The whole village will attend the funeral; and until it is over we will all think about death. There will be much headshaking and much spoiling of the children.

*

I do not own a watch and pass the summer without ever knowing the time. There is nothing to know it for, except the morning bus. Doña Anna's store is her house, and so is always open except for periods of sleep. Now and then, if the air is still enough, I can hear the chimes from the church clock wavering up to us, but never distinctly enough to count them. We have a crude measure of our own, however. As the sun rises, it projects through the top window and onto the white back wall a rectangle of orange light, which yellows and descends in the course of the morning. Thanks to a visiting watch, we have marked a crude scale on the wall — the first touch of light is approaching six o'clock, the top of the picture is nine, its bottom edge ten. It serves for the summer. I think I have twice missed the bus, but that may not have been the sun's fault, for Sebastián, unless he is forewarned, is apt to leave on whim, as long as there is at least one passenger for conversation. He, too, is watchless. And the church clock, bought by subscription six years ago, often veers ten minutes in either direction from the correct time, they tell me. But how do they know?

*

To live in the village, even temporarily, is to translate existence into a pure particularity. The silence is primordial, and the only sounds that violate it are those that I make myself. I grow more respectful of the natural world, and feel my presence as something of an intrusion. But I think of being there less as an escape than as a corrective; it gives me time to put my priorities in order. Although Spain has loomed large in my life, my specific attachment is to the village — to the children I have seen grow up and to the villagers I have watched grow old. However much one learns about and understands a country in terms of events, it is the lived experience that matters most, and I looked forward keenly to picking up the long, unfinished conversations, the view from the inside.

*

There is a sense in which all Spanish villages are interchangeable: they have in common a manner of being, a vantage point, and, in this present Spain, a plight. Having lived in four separate villages, I think I would feel at ease in any — in its rituals and hierarchies, in its dingy, loquacious café, in its human rhythm. Spanish villages bear to each other family likenesses. It is only when one gets to know a village by name — landscape, houses, people — that it becomes a quite separate drama, a web of connections and commitments, even of argument. Not that our village is ever rent by civic strife — it has waned considerably from its self-sustaining, self-regulating days, and is now administered bureaucratically from the anonymous outside as part of the region. Still, it generated its own garbage collection ahead of other villages, and the forces of law and order have had no cause to visit since local traffic in contraband stopped, except for one occasion, when a drink-crazed Norwegian ecologist let the air out of the tyres on the twenty-odd cars in the place, walking about four mountainous miles to do it.

To a village as small as ours, rituals are essential, and I go down the path in late morning to enact the rituals of arrival — the gnarled handshakes, the embraces, and the formal exchanges that might be scripted in stone. There is much headshaking and hand-wringing, accompanied by the gnomic sentences that seem so indigenous to the Spanish language, the natural proverbs that crop up in village conversations. Later on, I gather; bit by bit, all that has gone on in my absence, in many differing versions, variously edited by the tellers, and I put together the missing time, which is difficult, for the people here do not talk in years but in seasons, enumeration by weather and fruits and harvests. I listen a lot at first, and the happenings emerge — a forest fire, a death, a family feud — to fill in the gap in my time. It has been a winter of wind; but without much rain — alas, for the *cisternas* in the village are filled from the guttered roofs, and the supply of summer water depends on the ferocity of the winter rains. From May on, however, we do not talk of the weather, for it is steadily blue and hot and dry, with only infinitesimal variations. In summer, village life shifts down to half speed. Time stretches, people walk more slowly, everything moves in a sunstruck drift. May, however, has its surprises. I woke one morning early, to seemingly less light, and went out on the terrace to find myself in an eerie cold greyness. A cloud had settled on our small mountain, and I was standing in the middle of it, barely able to see the nearest almond tree. In under an hour, the sun had burned it away, but even in that short time I felt that I had been in and out of a separate season.

*

In the world of the village, death is a reduction, and among the old ones its inevitability sits like an attendant bird, like imminent nightfall. I feel the reduction more on this occasion, for during my absence Don Anselmo has died. His absence is almost as tangible as his presence, for it was he, more than anyone else, who gave the place a direction and a human shape. He had been mayor, as had his father, and he carried the annals of the place in his head, its past as vivid to him as its present. From his huge, worn armchair in the little *pensión* that he ran and where he was always to be found, he dispensed advice, stories, help, and unflagging kindness — something like a tribal headman, with a patient ear and an inexhaustible generosity of spirit. He had become so identified with the place that its well-being mattered more to him than his own, and I could not help feeling that with his death the spirit had gone out of it. I would often call on him in the late afternoon, and on this occasion, when that time of day came around, I felt at loose ends, I felt the deprivation of his death. One afternoon, I went down and collected the key to the small cemetery from the bar under the priest's house. I sat under a cypress tree, remembering an afternoon with Don Anselmo in that same spot, where he had told me about the other occupants of the sandstone niches, bringing them to life one by one. His own niche bears only his name and the legend '*Primera Y Última Morada*', first and last resting place. For Spaniards, death is neither a surprise nor a puzzle, since they invoke it so often in their daily conversation. As they approach it, they make of it a familiar, a silent companion to whom they look more and more. I find it easy, sitting here, to imagine Don Anselmo back into being, to play back a conversation with him, to hear his solemn voice recounting some part of the long narrative of the village. Now that he is dead, it is as though the place had suddenly lost its memory, as though all its annals lie there encased in stone, unreadable now, fading, buried.

*

It was during the sixties that I saw most of Don Anselmo. His wife knew both French and English and was an inveterate reader of magazines, which she summarized for Don Anselmo. It was thus that he became passionately interested in ecology, for he discovered that he had been its unwitting champion all his life. I once gave him a copy of *The Whole Earth Catalog*, and it was never far from his armchair. What excited him was the discovery that agricultural self-sufficiency and village-size communities were constantly invoked as ecological ideals, and he began more than ever to feel that the village of yesteryear had been something of an ecological Eden, if a threadbare one. Gravely, he began to advance schemes by which the village might give a further lead to the rest of the world. He tried to ban cars from the place, but since the old people depended on the bus, he relented. Our air, besides, is milk and honey. He proposed advertising for hippies to come and make fertile lately abandoned land, but he was dissuaded by some horrified foreign inhabitants. He considered bringing back the bartering of crops and goods, a ritual over which he had once presided, but since the only commodity that certain inhabitants could produce was money, he was again defeated by circumstance. He was always trying to think up small, productive enterprises for people in the village, but he could not prevent the drift toward the town, where the pickings were more immediate. In his later years, when the village ceased to be a working place and instead lived well enough off the leisure of others, a sadness grew about him, for his ideal had almost existed and, ironically, had been eroded by progress. Almost the last time I saw him, his conversation caused me to feel that he had given up and had equated the death of the village with his own. I remember well what he said. 'I have decided that what those learned people tell us about how we are using up the world, how we must live in harmony with what we have, has come too late for us. Perhaps it *could* have happened if we had heeded, but I do not think that it will happen now. Yet here we once lived just like that, although we no longer do. That pains me

— I find myself thinking more and more of those days, and wishing them back.' Some eight months later, I had a letter from my son, who was there at the time, telling me of Don Anselmo's death, and of his funeral, which brought out the whole population, and many from the region, in mourning for his huge lost presence and for the past he took with him. We do not stop at the *pensión* now, as we once did. As Eugenio once said, out of the air, 'I cannot bear to look at that empty armchair. It is too big for any of us.'

*

I have spent many days, in different years and seasons, alone in the house, as I am now, the silence huge and unbroken except by my own noises, by occasional birds and sheep bells, and sometimes by the fluting sound of children singing from the pinewoods across from the house, children from the summer retreat, out walking with an accompanying nun. Nobody comes, except by intention. Eugenio appears at odd times, to attend to the trees or to do the accounts. The almond crop is poor, he says — it was a winter of wind, not enough rain. I help him carry fertilizer down to the lower terrace, and then spend an hour or two clearing brush in the ilex forest behind the house. A cuckoo makes its slow way up the valley, loudmouthed against the quiet. I sit on the terrace and gaze. The edge of roof shadow is suddenly a foot closer to my chair. It is something I have always noticed about Spaniards — how so many of them sit in their own silence as though it were a bubble enclosing them, oblivious, wholly absorbed. Gerald Brenan writes about them, 'As they sit at their tables outside the cafés, their eyes record as on a photographic plate the people who are passing, but on a deeper level they are listening to themselves living.' It is something I absorb from the house, which seems to impose a silence of its own. I often think of it when I am far away from it: standing stony and empty, its eyes shuttered. I read, cook, draw water, write, gather wood, not according to plan but as these things occur to me, and from time to time I wander up through the forest, to lose myself, or to watch the late sun on the mountain across from it, changing the colours on its face, etching its shadows sharply. Music tinkles away below me in the neighbouring village, for they have there the beginnings of a rural disco. I walk slowly back through the ruins of the seven houses below ours, all that is left of the working hamlet it once was. Don Anselmo remembers it — remembered it. Now summer vegetation claws at the stones, and only our presence keeps it from taking over our house and similarly levelling it. It is natural, at the house, to think like a castaway, and it makes for stark thought.

*

Some of the foreigners who have come to rest in the village tell elaborate stories, carefully edited and well rubbed in the telling, of how they first stumbled on the place and forgot to leave. As my time here runs out, I think that they are not so farfetched, for the urgencies I have created for myself elsewhere seem trivial by now, and the timelessness I have grown into is something too rich to leave cursorily. But the day comes closer, inexorable as the shadow on the terrace, and I find myself looking at stones and trees as though for the last time, trying to fix the atmosphere of an afternoon like a print on my memory. Yet it is already imprinted there, from countless seasons and occasions, so completely that I can return to it in my head, in piercing detail. I know the stones marking the path as distinctly as faces, and a good number of the trees. I can summon up any time of day — the haze of early morning, the limpid, brilliant blue of noon, the ochre light following sunset that honeys the white wall. I can turn on the seasons — the drumming of the great rains, the white astonishment of the almond blossom in February, the pacific drowse of summer. I prowl through the house at will, fingering the talismans on the shelves and playing back sounds, footsteps on the path, the thud of fruit falling, the rattle of the bucket in the well. Most of all, I can in time induce the silence of the place, as an easement of mind. I suppose it has become for me what Gerard Manley Hopkins called an inscape, for although I can recall in like detail other places I have lived in, none have the same brilliance in my memory. I have the house and the forest in my head, out of time, and now to go back to it is only to confirm its existence. It and the village have been left behind, in a fold of time, and the new Spain might almost be another country. While it presses eagerly forward, the village looks wistfully back.

I take a last walk through the ilex forest, I pile up the newspapers in the niche by the fireplace, to yellow in their good time, I seal jars against the ants, I return to Eugenio the tools he has lent me, I prepare to close the house, as though it were a time capsule that will wait, sealed and safe, until I can open it up again. Except that, this time, I feel there is something of a difference. The house has stone walls at least two feet thick, and I have always felt that, short of a cataclysmic disaster, it would wait there, in its silence, for me to open it up again. This time, however, the hazards do not emanate from the ants, the termites, the clawing vegetation, the earthquakes, or the thunderbolts. The human world has become more precarious than the natural world, and I feel that I will owe my next return less to the obdurate, stony permanence of the house than to the restraint of our own wilful humanity, which has let us survive, however precariously, until now.

POEMS II

Curiosity

may have killed the cat. More likely,
the cat was just unlucky, or else curious
to see what death was like, having no cause
to go on licking paws, or fathering
litter on litter of kittens, predictably.

Nevertheless, to be curious
is dangerous enough. To distrust
what is always said, what seems,
to ask odd questions, interfere in dreams,
smell rats, leave home, have hunches,
does not endear cats to those doggy circles
where well-smelt baskets, suitable wives, good lunches
are the order of things, and where prevails
much wagging of incurious heads and tails.

Face it. Curiosity
will not cause us to die—
only lack of it will.
Never to want to see
the other side of the hill
or that improbable country
where living is an idyll
(although a probable hell)
would kill us all.
Only the curious
have if they live a tale
worth telling at all.

Dogs say cats love too much, are irresponsible,
are dangerous, marry too many wives,
desert their children, chill all dinner tables
with tales of their nine lives.
Well, they are lucky. Let them be
nine-lived and contradictory,
curious enough to change, prepared to pay
the cat-price, which is to die
and die again and again,
each time with no less pain.
A cat-minority of one
is all that can be counted on
to tell the truth; and what cats have to tell
on each return from hell
is this: that dying is what the living do,
that dying is what the loving do,
and that dead dogs are those who never know
that dying is what, to live, each has to do.

Propinquity

is the province of cats. Living by accident,
lapping the food at hand or sleeking down
in an adjacent lap when sleep occurs to them,
never aspiring to consistency
in homes or partners, unaware of property,
cats take their chances, love by need or nearness
as long as the need lasts, as long as the nearness

is near enough. The code of cats is simply
to take what comes. And those poor souls who claim
to own a cat, who long to recognize
in bland and narrowing eyes a look like love,
are bound to suffer should they expect
cats to come purring punctually home.
Home is only where the food and the fire are,
but might be anywhere. Cats fall on their feet,
nurse their own wounds, attend to their own laundry,
and purr at appropriate times. O folly, folly,
to love a cat, and yet
we dress with love the distance that they keep,
the hair-raising way they have, and easily blame
all their abandoned litters and torn ears
on some marauding tiger, well aware
that cats themselves do not care.

Yet part of us is cat. Confess—
love turns on accident and needs
nearness; and the various selves we have
accrue from our cat-wanderings, our chance
crossings. Imagination prowls at night,
cat-like, among odd possibilities.
Only our dog-sense brings us faithfully home,
makes meaning out of accident, keeps faith,
and, cat-and-dog, the arguments go at it.
But every night, outside, cat-voices call
us out to take a chance, to leave
the safety of our baskets and to let
what happens happen. 'Live, live!' they catcall.

'Each moment is your next! Propinquity,
propinquity is all!'

Cat-Faith

As a cat, caught by the door opening,
on the perilous top shelf, red-jawed and raspberry-
clawed,
lets itself fall floorward without looking,
sure by cat-instinct it will find the ground,
where innocence is; and falls
anyhow, in a furball, so fast that the eye
misses the twist and trust
that come from having fallen before,
and only notices cat silking away,
crime inconceivable in so meek a walk:

so do we let ourselves fall morningward
through shelves of dream. When, libertine at dark,
we let the visions in, and the black window
grotesques us back, our world unbalances.
Many-faced monsters of our own devising
jostle on the verge of sleep, as the room
loses its edges and grows hazed and haunted
by words murmured or by woes remembered,
till, sleep-dissolved, we fall, the known world leaves us,
and room and dream and self and safety melt
into a final madness, where any landscape
may easily curdle, and the dead cry out . . .

but ultimately, it ebbs. Voices recede.
The pale square of the window glows and stays.
Slowly the room arrives and dawns, and we
arrive in our selves. Last night, last week, the past
leak back, awake. As light solidifies,
dream dims. Outside, the washed hush of the garden
waits patiently and, newcomers from death,
how gratefully we draw its breath!
Yet, to endure that unknown night by night,
must we not be sure, with cat-insight,
we can afford its terrors, and that full day
will find us at the desk, sane, unafraid—
cheeks shaven, letters written, bills paid?

The O-Filler

One noon in the library, I watched a man—
imagine! — filling in O's, a little, rumpled
nobody of a man, who licked his stub of pencil
and leaned over every O with a loving care,
shading it neatly, exactly to its edges
until the open pages
were pocked and dotted with solid O's, like towns
and capitals on a map. And yet, so peppered,
the book appeared inhabited and complete.

That whole afternoon, as the light outside softened
and the library groaned woodenly,
he worked and worked, his o-so-patient shading

descending like an eyelid over each open O
for page after page. Not once did he miss one,
or hover even a moment over an *a*
or an *e* or a *p* or a *g*. Only the O's—
oodles of O's, O's multitudinous, O's manifold,
O's italic and roman.
And what light on his crumpled face when he
                                        discovered—
as I supposed — odd words like *zoo* and *ooze*,
polo, oolong and *odontology*!

Think now. In that limitless library,
all round the steep-shelved walls, bulging in their
                                        bindings,
books stood, waiting. Heaven knows how many
he had so far filled, but still there remained
uncountable volumes of O-laden prose, and odes
with inflated capital O's (in the manner of Shelley),
O-bearing Bibles and biographies,
even whole sections devoted to O alone,
all his for the filling. Glory, glory, glory!
How utterly open and endless the world must have
                                        seemed to him,
how round and ample! Think of it. A pencil
was all he needed. Life was one wide O.

And why, at the end of things, should O's not be
                                        closed
as eyes are? I envied him, for in my place
across the table from him, had I accomplished
anything as firm as he had, or as fruitful?

What could I show? A handful of scrawled lines,
an afternoon yawned and wondered away,
and a growing realization that in time
even my scribbled words would come
under his grubby thumb, and the blinds be drawn
on all my O's, with only this thought for comfort—
that when he comes to this poem, a proper joy
may amaze his wizened face and, O, a pure pleasure
make his relentless pencil quiver.

Mandala

THE PENIS MIGHTIER THAN

Counters

ounce	instant
dice	distant
trice	tryst
quartz	catalyst
quince	quest
sago	sycamore
serpent	sophomore
oxygen	oculist
nitrogen	novelist
denim	dentist
acreage	archery
brokerage	butchery
cribbage	treachery
carthage	taproom
cage	tomb
sink	sermon
sentiment	cinnamon
ointment	apron
nutmeg	nunnery
doom	density

Oddments, Inklings, Omens, Moments

Oddments, as when
you see through skin,
when flowers appear
to be eavesdropping,
or music somewhere
declares your mood;
when sleep fulfils
a feel of dying
or fear makes ghosts
of clothes on a chair.

Inklings, as when
some room rhymes
with a lost time,
or a book reads
like a well-known dream;
when a smell recalls
portraits, funerals,
when a wish happens
or a mirror sees
through distances.

Omens, as when
a shadow from nowhere
falls on a wall,
when a bird seems
to mimic your name,
when a cat eyes you
as though it knew

or, heavy with augury,
a crow caws
cras cras from a tree.

Moments, as when
the air's awareness
makes guesses true,
when a hand's touch
speaks past speech
or when, in poise,
two sympathies
lighten each other,
and love occurs
like song, like weather.

An Instance

Perhaps the accident of a bird
crossing the green window, a simultaneous phrase
of far singing, and a steeplejack
poised on the church spire, changing the gold clock,
set the moment alight. At any rate, a word
in that instant of realizing catches fire,
ignites another, and soon the page is ablaze
with a wildfire of writing. The clock chimes in the
                                          square.

All afternoon, in a scrawl of time,
the mood still smoulders. Rhyme remembers rhyme,
and words summon the moment when amazement

ran through the senses like a flame.
Later, the song forgotten, the sudden bird
flown who-knows-where, the incendiary word
long since crossed out, the steeplejack gone home,
their moment burns again, restored
to its spontaneity. The poem stays.

A Lesson in Music

Play the tune again: but this time
with more regard for the movement at the source of it
and less attention to time. Time falls
curiously in the course of it.

Play the tune again: not watching
your fingering, but forgetting, letting flow
the sound till it surrounds you. Do not count
or even think. Let go.

Play the tune again: but try to be
nobody, nothing, as though the pace
of the sound were your heart beating, as though
the music were your face.

Play the tune again. It should be easier
to think less every time of the notes, of the measure.
It is all an arrangement of silence. Be silent, and then
play it for your pleasure.

Play the tune again; and this time, when it ends,
do not ask me what I think. Feel what is happening

strangely in the room as the sound glooms over
you, me, everything.

Now,
play the tune again.

Directions for a Map

Birds' eyes see almost this, a tiny island
odd as a footprint on a painted sea.
But maps set margins. Here, the land is measured,
changed to a flat, explicit world of names.

Crossing the threads of roads to nibbled coastlines,
the rivers run in veins that crack the surface.
Mountains are dark like hair, and here and there
lakes gape like moth holes with the sea showing through.

Between the seaports stutter dotted shiplines,
crossing designs of latitude and language.
The towns are flying names. The sea is titled.
A compass crowns the corner like a seal.

Distance is spelt in alphabets and numbers.
Arrows occur at intervals of inches.
There are no signs for love or trouble, only
dots for a village and a cross for churches.

Here space is free for once from time and weather.
The sea has paused. To plot is possible.

Given detachment and a careful angle,
all destinations are predictable.

And given, too, the confidence of distance,
strangers may take a hundred mural journeys.
For once the paths are permanent, the colours
outlast the seasons and the deaths of friends.

And even though, on any printed landscape,
directions never tell you where to go,
maps are an evening comfort to the traveller—
a pencil line will quickly take him home.

The Academy

I do not think of the academy
in the whirl of days. It does not change. I do.
The place hangs in my past like an engraving.
I went back once to lay a wreath on it,
and met discarded selves I scarcely knew.

It has a lingering aura, leather bindings,
a smell of varnish and formaldehyde,
a certain dusty holiness in the cloisters.
We used to race our horses on the sand
away from it, manes flying, breathing hard.

Trailing to the library of an afternoon,
we saw the ivy crawling underneath
the labyrinthine bars on the window ledges.

I remember the thin librarian's look of hate
as we left book holes in her shelves, like missing teeth.

On evenings doomed by bells, we felt the sea
creep up, we heard the temperamental gulls
wheeling in clouds about the kneeworn chapel.
They keened on the knifing wind like student souls.
Yet we would dent the stones with our own footfalls.

Students still populate the place, bright starlings,
their notebooks filled with scribbled parrot-answers
to questions they unravel every evening
in lamplit pools of spreading argument.
They slash the air with theory, like fencers.

Where is the small, damp-browed professor now?
Students have pushed him out to sea in a boat
of lecture-notes. Look, he bursts into flame!
How glorious a going for one whose words
had never struck a spark on the whale-road.

And you will find retainers at their posts,
wearing their suits of age, brass buttons, flannel,
patrolling lawns they crop with careful scissors.
They still will be in silver-haired attendance
to draw lines through our entries in the annals.

It is illusion, the academy.
In truth, the ideal talking-place to die.
Only the landscape keeps a sense of growing.
The towers are floating on a shifting sea.
You did not tell the truth there, nor did I.

Think of the process — moments becoming poems
which stiffen into books in the library,
and later, lectures, books about the books,
footnotes and dates, a stone obituary.
Do you wonder that I shun the academy?

It anticipates my dying, turns to stone
too quickly for my taste. It is a language
nobody speaks, refined to ritual:
the precise writing on the blackboard wall,
the drone of requiem in the lecture hall.

I do not think much of the academy
in the drift of days. It does not change. I do.
This poem will occupy the library
but I will not. I have not done with doing.
I did not know the truth there, nor did you.

Growing, Flying, Happening

Say the soft bird's name, but do not be surprised
to see it fall
headlong, struck skyless, into its pigeonhole—
columba palumbus and you have it dead,
wedged, neat, unwinged in your head.

That that black-backed tatter-winged thing
straking the harbour water and then plummeting
down, to come up, sleek head-a-cock,
a minted herring shining in its beak,
is a *guillemot*, is neither here nor there

in the amazement of its rising,
wings slicing the stiff salt air.

That of that spindling spear-leaved plant,
wearing the palest purple umbel,
many-headed, blue-tinted, stilt-stalked
at the stream-edge, one should say briefly
angelica, is by-the-way (though grant
the name itself to be beautiful).
Grant too that any name
makes its own music, that *bryony, sally-my-handsome*
burst at their sound into flower,
and that *falcon* and *phalarope* fly off in the ear,
still,
names are for saying at home.

The point is seeing — the grace
beyond recognition, the ways
of the bird rising, unnamed, unknown,
beyond the range of language, beyond its noun.
Eyes open on growing, flying, happening,
and go on opening. Manifold, the world
dawns on unrecognizing, realizing eyes.
Amazement is the thing.
Not love, but the astonishment of loving.

Poem Without Ends

One cannot take the beginning out of the air
saying 'It is the time: the hour is here.'

The process is continuous as wind,
the bird observed, not rising, but in flight,
unrealized, in motion in the mind.

The end of everything is similar, never
actually happening, but always over.
The agony, the bent head, only tell
that already in the heart the innocent evening
is thick with all the ferment of farewell.

Weathering

I am old enough now for a tree
once planted, knee high, to have grown to be
twenty times me,

and to have seen babies marry, and heroes grow deaf—
but that's enough meaning-of-life.
It's living through time we ought to be connoisseurs of.

From wearing a face all this time, I am made aware
of the maps faces are, of the inside wear and tear.
I take to faces that have come far.

In my father's carved face, the bright eye
he sometimes would look out of, seeing a long way
through all the tree-rings of his history.

I am awed by how things weather: an oak mantel
in the house in Spain, fingered to a sheen,
the marks of hands leaned into the lintel,

the tokens in the drawer I sometimes touch—
a crystal lived-in on a trip, the watch
my father's wrist wore to a thin gold sandwich.

It is an equilibrium
that breasts the cresting seasons but still stays calm
and keeps warm. It deserves a good name.

Weathering. Patina, gloss, and whorl.
The trunk of the almond tree, gnarled but still fruitful.
Weathering is what I would like to do well.

Neruda and Borges

When I first went to Spain, in 1953, I knew little about the living country and barely a word of the language. But my senses were in good working order, and I was instantly drawn in by Spain's rhythms and its landscapes — the burned, sun-stained earth, the silver-blue clarity of Mediterranean light, the warm solemnity of the people, the spareness of village life. Existence was honed down to its essentials, making the days longer, time more abundant. So I returned to Spain, and returned, and eventually went to live there in 1956, setting out to learn the country, and slowly absorb the Spanish sense of time. Spaniards have a gift for expanding the present, around a meal or a conversation; and they are masters of the cosmic shrug that sheds all preoccupations except those immediately at hand. But living in Spain meant, above all, entering the Spanish language, for in those early days I felt separated from the spoken life around me, a bafflement hard to bear. Spanish, at first encounter, is welcoming: you enter it by way of the market and the kitchen, but you soon find yourself stranded on that plateau of daily needs. The language lies still beyond. Living in another language means growing another self, and it takes time for that other self to become a familiar. While I went about learning the machinery and the music, I realized at the same time that the Spanish I was acquiring was as devoid of context as that of a young child, for I had no past in the language. I was lucky, however, in having wise friends, and, following their counsel, I entered a continuum of reading and listening.

There is nothing like immersion in an unknown — new places, new landscapes, new preoccupations, new loves, a new language — to sharpen the edge of attention. From Majorca, where I first landed, I moved to Madrid and then to Barcelona. I travelled all over — to the Basque country, to Andalusia, to Gibraltar and Morocco, to Portugal — looking and listening a lot, and I wrote the first of a series of chronicles on Spain for *The New Yorker*. Soon after it appeared, I had my Spanish press credentials withdrawn, but that made little difference, for Spain existed then on rumour and speculation. Living there felt like belonging to an extensive whispered conspiracy against the Franco regime. Spain was at something of a standstill, still in shock from the Civil War and the long isolation that followed it, threadbare compared to the rest of Europe. Censorship, both moral and political, hung heavy over the press, over the universities, and over writers and publishers, and the police had sharp antennae out for any sign of dissidence. The writers I knew complained that years of censorship had instilled in Spaniards the habit of censoring themselves. Newspapers were grey and evasive, written opinion was sparse and guarded, and literature was thin and spare.

Among my friends in Barcelona was a young poet and publisher named Carlos Barral, lean, birdlike, throaty-voiced, and given to infectious enthusiasms. Carlos's imprint, Seix Barral, published the work of new Spanish writers and of European writers in translation, and consequently was always battling the censor. Carlos's enthusiasm at that time, however, was for the writing that was beginning to appear from the countries of Spanish America. In 1962, he published Mario Vargas Llosa's novel *La Ciudad y los Perros*, later translated as *The Time of the Hero*. The book was received in Spain with an excitement hardly ever generated by the Spanish novels of the day, and it led Carlos to proclaim, with remarkable prescience, that it was from the countries of Spanish America that we should expect not just the next literary flowering but the renewing of the Spanish language.

In those days, the attitude of Spaniards toward Spanish America most resembled the way the English used to regard the United States, with an insufferable condescension. Europe was much more immediate to them than the South American continent, and their knowledge of it was vague. So was mine. I had in my head a mixture of school geography, Hollywood epics, Carmen Miranda with fruit on her head, paeons asleep under huge sombreros, the bossa nova, and the chachacha. It may have had something to do with the stasis of Spain at the time, but, through the books and manuscripts that Carlos passed on to me — books like Juan Rulfo's *Pedro Páramo* and Alejo Carpentier's *The Lost Steps* — I began to take an impassioned interest in South America, and to read its turbulent history with some amazement. More than that, I found in the literature a loosening of Spanish from its Castilian restraints, an intense verbal energy. I noticed the same thing in the few Spanish Americans I came across in Barcelona: they had more exuberance than we were used to in Spain and, given the occasion, they turned conversation on its ear, making a playground of the language.

When Mario Vargas Llosa came to Barcelona, Carlos introduced me. Mario had left Peru behind and lived in Paris, working for the French radio network: he broadcast to Latin America at night and wrote by day. He had a kind of flashing intensity to him, and a single, burning ambition: to live by his writing. It was nearly impossible, he said, to make a living as a writer in Latin America: editions were small, readers were sparse, and few writers were read beyond their own borders, since tariff barriers in many countries made books hard to come by. While the separate countries of Latin America all had their writers, it made little sense, Mario said, to speak of a 'Latin American' literature. As yet, there was no body of writing that had found its way through translation into other literatures and so achieved international recognition. Within a decade, that was to change utterly, with the surge of memorable novels, popularly referred to as the Boom, that appeared in the aftermath of the Cuban Revolution of 1959 and received great acclaim in many languages: novels by Vargas Llosa, Julio Cortázar, Gabriel García Márquez, José Donoso, Alejo Carpentier, and Guillermo Cabrera Infante. Prior to that eruption, however, very few writers from Spanish America had earned international attention. Foremost among them were the Chilean poet Pablo Neruda and the Argentine master Jorge Luis Borges. They were, each in a quite separate way, the forerunners of the writers of the Boom.

I had been introduced to Borges's writing a few years earlier, by Pipina Prieto, a vivacious Argentine who had known him in Buenos Aires and who spoke of him with such fervour that when she pressed his *Ficciones* on me I would not have dared not read it. The effect on an unsuspecting reader of encountering a work of Borges's can be alarming enough almost to justify a publisher's warning on the book jacket. His stories induce a kind of vertigo in his readers, an eerie after-effect that can invest small happenings, like breaking a glass or missing a train, with ominous significance. Pipina was a bewitching talker, and could practically perform Borges's stories. We talked them over, endlessly, and before long I kept the half-dozen slender books that contained most of his writing then — poems and essays as well as stories — always at hand.

I had been coming across the poetry of Neruda piecemeal, mostly in the houses of friends, for Neruda's books were then proscribed in Spain as Communist literature. There is an extraordinary lift that comes from reading Neruda's poetry for the first time: both from its sheer beauty on the ear and from its great tumble of images. But I found not one but many Nerudas. I read his fierce elegies on the Spanish Civil War, and his tender, whimsical 'Ode to My Socks', his sensual love poems, and the high incantatory pitch of his *Heights of Machu Picchu*, and I wondered at their accomplished variety but had no sense, yet, of who the poet was among so many incarnations.

That these two writers should be acclaimed as the quintessential Spanish-American writers of their time was particularly intriguing to me, for the more I read them the more I felt them to be about as different from each other, as writers and as human souls, as it is possible to be. Borges's work is as spare as Neruda's is ebullient, as dubious and ironic as Neruda's is passionately affirmative, as reticent as Neruda's is voluble. Where Neruda is open, even naïve, Borges is oblique and sceptical; where Neruda is a sensualist, a poet of physical love, a man of appetites, Borges is an ascetic; where Neruda is rooted in what he has experienced, Borges seems to have lived almost entirely in literature, in the mind-travel of his reading. Borges accepted being Argentine as his destiny, Buenos Aires as his locality, but his preoccupations were wholly metaphysical. Where Neruda in his poems addressed the realities of the Latin-American present and lived on intimate terms with the physical world, Borges's writings often cast doubt on the very existence of that world, except as a mental projection, a fiction.

*

Borges was born in 1899, in the Buenos Aires suburb of Palermo, into a middle-class professional family: his father was a lawyer and a teacher of psychology with literary aspirations, his mother a descendant of military heroes and Argentine patriots. From an early age, the son was seen by the family as destined to become a writer, fulfilling the ambitions of his father, whose literary career had been stayed by encroaching blindness — a hereditary blindness, which was to descend on Borges gradually from his late twenties. In 1914, the whole family moved to Europe, where they lived for the next seven years — first in Geneva, where Borges studied and read French and German, and then in Spain, where he began to write in earnest. When he returned to Argentina, in 1921, fired by a new enthusiasm for his country, he began a literary career — as a poet, an essayist, and a reviewer, in the world of salons, *tertulias*, and small magazines — that continued all his life.

Neruda had his beginnings in 1904, in Parral, in the rainy south of Chile, where his father worked on the railroad, on the frontier of the great forests. He has recreated his solitary, awestruck childhood, his discovery of the secret life of words, in a number of enchanted poems. Luck seemed to attend him early.

His first poems were brought to the attention of the Chilean poet Gabriela Mistral, and she helped him gain a scholarship to study French in Santiago when he was seventeen. In the capital, he moved from the absorbed solitude of adolescence into an artist's underworld of close friendships, nightlong conversations, sexual love, and the poems of Rimbaud and Baudelaire. It was a heady transformation. Neruda's *Twenty Love Poems and a Song of Despair*, published in 1924 (written in that flush of late adolescence), became, and still are, a kind of touchstone for first love, learned by heart everywhere in the Spanish-speaking world. 'I have been marking the blank chart of your body,' Neruda writes in one of them, 'with crosses of fire / My mouth was a spider that scuttles into hiding / In you, behind you, tremulous and thirsty.' These poems are remarkable in their erotic intensity, in their startling sensual directness.

Such early fame led to Neruda's being appointed, in that most enlightened of Latin-American traditions, to the Chilean Consular Service, and between the ages of twenty-three and twenty-eight he was posted in turn to Rangoon, Ceylon, Java, and Singapore. The five years Neruda was away from Chile were a difficult time for him, separated from his language and his roots; yet out of his loneliness and alienation came the cumulative volumes of *Residencia en la Tierra* (*Sojourn on Earth*) — hallucinatory poems in which, deprived of his own country, he creates wildly surreal landscapes out of his own private obsessions, with a poetic density quite startlingly new to poetry in

Spanish. When he returned to Chile, his fame as a poet had spread so widely that, posted to Spain in 1934, he was acclaimed by the community of Spanish poets, Federico García Lorca and Miguel Hernández among them. But these were the last euphoric days of the Republic. When the Civil War broke out, Neruda remained in Spain, but the experience marked him forever. His friend García Lorca was sought out and shot, and everywhere about him Neruda saw Spain broken. The war brought about in him a deep political conversion. He was asked to resign his consulship because of his outspoken sympathy for the Republic. The poems he wrote at that time are bitter in their anger.

> Generals,
> traitors,
> look at my dead house,
> look at broken Spain:
> out of every dead house comes burning
>   metal
> instead of flowers,
> out of every crater in Spain
> Spain reappears,
> out of every dead child comes a rifle
>   with eyes,
> every crime breeds bullets
> that will one day find their way
> to your heart.

You will ask why don't his poems
tell us of dreams, of leaves,
of the great volcanoes of his homeland?

Come and see the blood in the streets.
come and see
the blood in the streets,
come and see the blood
in the streets!

Back in Chile, Neruda, still haunted by his Spanish experience, joined the Chilean Communist Party, and in 1945 was elected to the Chilean Senate, plunging into an active political life. After he published, in 1947, an open letter criticizing President Gabriel González Videla, he was forced into hiding for an extended period to avoid arrest, and was sheltered in different houses until he could escape over the Andes to Argentina. Out of that came his *Canto General,* an enormous hymn to Latin America — its exotic geography, its cruel history, its brutal politics, and its present human wrongs — in a sprawling mass of poems. The book, published in 1950, had an immense impact, more political than poetic. Besides the overtly political poems, however, it contained a sequence of visionary cantos he called *Alturas de Machu Picchu* (*The Heights of Machu Picchu*). He had visited the Inca shrine in 1943, and these impassioned invocations contain Neruda's poetic creed. He sees Machu Picchu as built on the bones of centuries of oppressed Indians, and he vows to become a voice for all things that have no voice, to speak out for the oppressed of the past and against the oppressions of the present. In this new writing, Neruda abandoned the surreal extravagance of his earlier work, and thenceforth deliberately simplified his poetry, to make it accessible to the people of Chile who gave him shelter in their houses as a fugitive. In Chile, he was now a national possession.

*

Alongside such a crowded existence, Borges's life appears singularly static. On his return to Buenos Aires from Europe, he set about rediscovering his native city, first in poems and then in a series of incisive essays on Argentine themes. His world was a purely literary one; he regularly reviewed foreign literature, and translated works of Virginia Woolf, Kafka, Joyce, and Faulkner into Spanish. But his brief literary essays were often oblique and unconventional: with time, a certain playful element showed itself — in quotations ascribed to nonexistent originals, citations of imaginary authors. Although Borges was not writing fiction, he began to intrude fictional elements into his other writings. He used to say that he considered scholarship merely a branch of fantastic literature. He told me once that as a young man he had contemplated writing a long dynastic novel encompassing the history of Argentina since independence, until he realized that he could write, in the span of a few pages, a descriptive review of just such a work by an invented author, adding his reflections on the genre. It was not until 1939, following first the death of his father and then a long convalescence after a near-fatal accident, that he began to write the disquieting stories that were published in 1944 as *Ficciones* — the stories that brought him fame far beyond Argentina.

It is somewhat deceptive to talk of Borges as a storyteller, as a poet, or as an essayist, however, for he blurred these divisions by exploring the same paradoxes in the varying forms of story, poem, and essay. To him they are all 'fictions' — words on a page, constructs of the mind. Borges concludes his epilogue to *El Hacedor*, a collection he published in 1960, with the following:

> A man sets himself the task of drawing the world.
> As the years pass, he fills the empty space with images of provinces and kingdoms, mountains, bays, ships, islands, fish, houses, instruments, stars, horses, and people. Just before he dies, he discovers that the patient labyrinth of lines traces the image of his own face.

Such fictions are Borges's trademark. From the sixties on, Borges's reputation spread with the speed of a virus through the reading world, infecting it with a sly, humorous scepticism about language, about all matters literary. His writings are deeply subversive — by implication, they call into question all linguistic versions of everything. In whatever Borges writes he never lets his readers forget that what they hold in their hands is a text, a fiction made of words, from a fallible mind. The natural world remains fearful and incomprehensible to us; to contend with it, to give it order and purpose, the mind creates fictions — fables, histories, rules, codes of law, theories, social systems, predictions, even divinities. However 'perfect' these fictions might be, reality defies them by remaining chaotic and unpredictable. Yet the making of fictions is essential to our nature: literature, Borges insists, is our solace.

In 1961, Borges shared with Samuel Beckett the Prix International des Éditeurs, which led to immediate translation of his stories into the main European languages. Anthony Kerrigan, who was editing *Ficciones* in English, asked me to translate the story 'Tlön, Uqbar, Orbis Tertius'. By then, I had come to know and appreciate Borges's uncharacteristic prose style — a style that is spare, restrained, and carefully formal, and uses something like understatement, not exactly a characteristic of written Spanish. While I worked I had the curious feeling that I was retranslating something back into English that had previously been translated into Spanish. Most crucial to me was to catch the tone — tentative, wary, uncertain — in which Borges writes, a manner that constantly questions what it is telling, sometimes by tone alone.

'Tlön, Uqbar, Orbis Tertius' begins with Borges's discovery, through a chance remark by a friend, of an item in a corrupt encyclopedia about an enigmatic region called Uqbar. The region is apparently fictitious.

'Reading it over,' Borges says characteristically, 'we discovered, beneath the superficial authority of the prose, a fundamental vagueness.' Some time later, in a remote hotel, chance puts into Borges's hands a volume of another encyclopedia, devoted to a vast planet called Tlön. A trail of further clues reveals that a group of seventeenth-century sages originally conceived the idea of creating an entirely rational planet — one that would be wholly comprehensible to its inhabitants — and of disseminating knowledge of it by way of a secret encyclopedia. A postscript to the story, set at a future date, describes how the human race eventually embraces the world of Tlön as though it were reality. Objects from Tlön begin to turn up in the real world, and, as in many of Borges's stories, reality gives way to a wished-for fiction.

For Borges, rational systems that are extended to the extreme limits of their rationality turn into nightmare. In his 'The Library of Babel', a 'total' library is obliged to contain not only all actual books but all possible books as well. The entire world becomes a library. In 'The Babylon Lottery', set in an imagined past of Babylon, an apparently rational society elects to introduce some element of chance into its existence by starting a lottery. Bit by bit, to increase the excitement, the numbers of the lottery are made to signify not just prizes but punishments — fines, imprisonment, even execution. The mysterious company administering the lottery is eventually suspected of being a fiction. Babylon gives itself over completely to chance, and order yields irresistibly to chaos.

*

Neruda and Borges met only once, in July of 1927, in Buenos Aires. Following the success of *Twenty Love Poems*, Neruda, then turning twenty-three, was on his way to take up his first diplomatic appointment, as Chilean consul in Rangoon. Borges, at twenty-seven, had published two volumes of poems and was an active reviewer in the literary magazines of the day. The meeting was one that each of them described in later life: they recalled that they had talked about the unsatisfactory nature of Spanish, and the resignation they both felt at having to write in it. The one enthusiasm they shared was for the poems of Walt Whitman, whose work both of them had translated. The meeting appears to have been more diplomatic than intimate, and they went to some trouble to avoid meeting again. It seems to have occurred to each of them that they had little in common as writers except the Spanish language; as time went on, they were often asked about each other, and in their responses they were most of the time polite and respectful, no more. Borges regarded their meeting as essentially nonserious. Neruda was more specific. In a letter to an Argentine friend he wrote:

> Borges, whom you mention, seems to me over-preoccupied with those problems of culture and

society which do not attract me, which are not *human*. I prefer the great wines, love, suffering, and books as a consolation for the inevitable solitude. I even feel a certain scorn for culture as a way of interpreting things. I prefer sure awareness without precedent, a physical absorption in the world ... History, the problems of 'knowledge', as they are called, seem to me lacking in dimension. How much of it would it take to fill the void? I see around me always fewer ideas, always more bodies, sunshine and sweat. I am exhausted.

For all their youthful excess, Neruda's observations, about himself in particular, are remarkably clear. He remained entirely a poet of the physical world, a materialist, actually as well as politically: he had no interest in metaphysical questions, and disliked literary talk. He did not write his poems for literary circles: he wanted them out in the street, read by everyday inhabitants of the language. He achieved just that, in his own time, as has no other poet I can think of. He accomplished what Whitman only aspired to; he became what Whitman had hoped to be.

Borges, on the other hand, remained remote, indecipherable to many: it requires a certain nerve even to try to follow the quirks of his mind. In a celebrated essay, 'Kafka and His Precursors', he makes the point that after reading Kafka we recognize foreshadowings of him in the work of writers who preceded him in time, and we refer to them as Kafkaesque. As Borges wrote, 'The fact is that every writer *creates* his own precursors. His work modifies our conception of the past, as it will modify the future.' This is precisely what has happened in Borges's case. Certain intrusions of disquiet that undermine a believed reality are so much a mark of his mind and manner that when we find the same dismaying twists in writers who preceded him in time we refer to these twists as Borgesian.

It may well have been the intense appeal of Borges's writings to academics in all languages that made him such an intrusive literary figure. Books about him abound, theses and critical studies multiply: unravelling Borges is something of an industry. Neruda, to the contrary, has attracted comparatively little critical study: the great mass of his poetry is simply there, always accessible, like the ocean.

*

The more I read my way into Spanish America, the more I felt my ignorance of it as a living place. When a piece of time suddenly opened for me in early 1964, I bought a round-trip ticket from New York to Buenos Aires that allowed me an unlimited number of linear stops. I made many. I met a whole web of writers, and they passed me on from one country to friends in the next. I made solitary pilgrimages to shrines like Chichen Itzá and Machu Picchu, but otherwise, wherever I went, I found myself in the middle of a seemingly endless conversation that ranged all the way from pure play to high art. I asked a lot of questions, but mostly I listened.

In mid-February, I landed into a golden summer in Chile. Someone had given me a letter to Jorge Elliot, a painter and art critic in Santiago, and I called on him soon after arriving. He welcomed me as though I had been expected, and invited me to a summer house he had in Isla Negra, the village on the Pacific Coast where Neruda then lived.

Isla Negra was little more than a string of houses built along a low cliff above a broad beach where the Pacific thundered incessantly. The families who lived there knew each other well, and the place had a well-worn, easygoing air. Neruda had settled there in the fifties, in a house perched on the cliff, and he had added to it eccentrically as money came in, book by book. Beside the house stood a ship's yardarm, and as we approached it Jorge pointed out a small blue flag flying from it. 'Pablo's at home,' he said.

Neruda's garden was dominated by a steamroller that he had rescued, painted, and installed as a shrine. Under the yardarm, a boat was grounded, geraniums growing from its stem, and beyond it lay an anchor, all of them like props from Neruda's poems. We went inside, and into a high-ceilinged living room with stone walls, a fireplace framed by granite boulders from the beach, and a wooden gallery with stairs descending. Objects were everywhere: ships' figureheads leaning out of the corners; driftwood; shells; tackle; books. On a long, heavy table under a wide window that framed the Pacific lay more objects: a ship under glass; a sextant; a telescope; odd-shaped bottles; agates gathered from the beach. The light in the room wavered with the white of the breaking waves below. The house might have been afloat. Suddenly, Neruda called out, and came down from the gallery, a captain descending from his bridge.

He was a large man — portly, even — but majestic and deliberate in his movement. His eyes were large and hooded, rather like those of a bemused lizard, and seemed to take in everything, but slowly. He moved slowly, turned his head slowly, blinked slowly; and when he spoke his voice, mellowly resonant, was close to languid. His words had the weight of stones. I noticed, then and whenever I later met him, that, since he was generally the centre of attention, he had a way of slowing down everything around him, pacing the conversation. As he talked, he moved about the room, touching a surface here, picking up an agate from the table and gazing into it, entranced. The objects were a kind of vocabulary: the collections of shells, of ships in bottles, of French postcards, of clocks and hats and walking sticks; a huge wooden shoe he had badgered from a bootmaker; a full-sized papier-mâché horse.

Thinking of Neruda, I still see him in that house: it was an externalization of his whole being. He used to say that he had a secondary profession, as a surreal architect, a transformer of houses. He required of his houses that they be in remarkable places, that they have space for all the multifarious objects he brought back from his travels, that they have a workroom for his writing, and that they be comfortable, humorous, and accessible to his friends. Each house was his private theatre, where he had designed the sets and always played the lead.

Neruda was then in his sixtieth year, and, in anticipation of his birthday, he had written *Memorial de Isla Negra*, an autobiography in the form of more than a hundred poems, divided into five sections, each covering a stage of his life. The galley proofs were draped along the back of a sofa. He was also translating *Romeo and Juliet* for performance later that year, and he asked me several questions about the text. Neruda was glum about his translation; English and Spanish did such different things, he said, they were really misfits. After some translation tinkering, we moved outside, to a long table adjoining the kitchen, where Neruda's wife, Matilde Urrutia, came to join us.

In the presence of food and drink, Neruda always expanded visibly. On this occasion, he brought the sheaf of galleys to the table, and at a replete pause he read to us, in that mesmerizing voice, carefully phrased, that seemed to float the poem in the air. I had no inkling of it then, but seventeen years later I was to translate that book in its entirety, poem by poem.

Later that night, I talked with Jorge about Neruda. He found for me a copy of Neruda's brief prose manifesto *On Impure Poetry.*

It is very appropriate, at certain times of the day or night, to look deeply into objects at rest: wheels which have traversed vast dusty spaces, bearing great cargoes of vegetables or minerals, sacks from the coal yards, barrels, baskets, the handles and grips of the carpenter's tools. They exude the touch of man and the earth as a lesson to the tormented poet. Worn surfaces, the mark hands have left on things, the aura, sometimes tragic and always wistful, of these objects lend to reality a fascination not to be taken lightly.

The flawed confusion of human beings shows in them, the proliferation, materials used and discarded, the prints of feet and fingers, the permanent mark of humanity on the inside and outside of all objects.

That is the kind of poetry we should be after, poetry worn away as if by acid by the labour of hands, impregnated with sweat and smoke, smelling of lilies and of urine, splashed by the variety of what we do, legally or illegally.

A poetry as impure as old clothes, as a body, with its foodstains and its shame, with wrinkles, observations, dreams, wakefulness, prophecies, declarations of love and hate, stupidities, shocks, idylls, political beliefs, negations, doubts, affirmations, taxes.

I went back along the sand path to Neruda's house

several times. He and I combed the beach for agates at the ebb, laughed a lot, talked a lot, ate and drank exuberantly well. Since I wore no shoes, Pablo and Matilde called me, then and ever after, Patapelá (Barefoot), and when I said my farewells Pablo gave me a volume of his, *Estravagario*. We made promises to meet again, somewhere, sometime. Such a meeting seemed to me improbable; but then so did being in Chile, that long, thin, bountiful country.

When I left, I flew to Mendoza, at the foot of the Andes on the Argentine side, and, with two days to wait for the train across the pampas to Buenos Aires, I made notes and read, Isla Negra still vivid in my head. The trees in Mendoza's elegant small squares were shedding their leaves, and under a limpid blue sky the dark wall of the Andes towered in the piercing clarity of the air. It felt to me like Shangri-La.

*

Buenos Aires has always struck me as the most sumptuous of cities: the abundance of its shops and restaurants made Madrid and Barcelona then seem frugal by comparison, and in its well-stocked bookstores I bought the books forbidden us in Spain — principally Neruda's *Collected Poems*, a Losada volume, on India paper, of a thousand nine hundred and thirty-two pages. Very little of Buenos Aires seemed Spanish. Listening to conversations in that assured *porteño* accent, I felt that the Spanish language had now detached itself from Spain, and had taken on many different modes. After a day or two of exploring, I telephoned Borges at the National Library where he had been director since 1955. Pipina had written ahead to him, and had given me his number.

He came on the line, and, on identifying me, he changed to his very courteous English and asked me to call on him in the library that afternoon. When I arrived, I was directed by a guard to Borges's office. I must have misheard, for I found myself in the deeper twilit recesses of the library, lost. I might almost have expected it. An assistant rescued me and led me to where Borges sat, at the end of a long library table, a pile of books at hand, in a pool of light cast by the lamp. He rose to greet me, his face upturned toward the sound of my voice.

That meeting, the first of many, so imprinted itself on me that each time I met Borges I felt I was reenacting it. It came in part from his blindness, which meant that one had to find one's way to him, a presence, waiting patiently. To exist for him, people had to come within his earshot, into the pool of his attention, a pool that encompassed a library of blind volumes, all of Borges's memory, all he had read and thought, all he had written and would write. To meet him was to be admitted to the universe of his blindness, to the crowded solitude he inhabited, to the still pool of his attention.

There was something frail about his company — the soft, quiet voice, the conceded vulnerability of his blindness. He mostly spoke to me in English, which he had learned as a child from his paternal grandmother, an Englishwoman of Northumbrian stock — Borges's English had a faint northern cast to it. As he explained once in an interview, 'When I was talking to my paternal grandmother I had to speak in a manner that I afterwards discovered was called English, and when I was talking to my mother or her parents I had to talk a language that afterwards turned out to be Spanish.' It was in English that he read first, in his father's library. He thought of English ever after as the language of culture, Spanish as the language his mother spoke in the kitchen to the servants, the language of the street and the outside world. He spoke English with the respect due a language he knew well but did not live in: he spoke in the careful cadence of books. On other occasions, in Spanish-speaking company, he would become much more mischievous, less solemn. Yet I think it was the very fact of his bilingual upbringing that gave him his acute sense of the arbitrary and deceptive nature of language: a bilingual is much more aware of the gulf between word and thing than someone confined to a single language.

Irony accompanied Borges like a familiar, present not only in everything he wrote but also in so many of the circumstances of his life: in the family's understanding that he would become a writer and yet would probably succumb to the congenital blindness that had afflicted his father and five preceding generations; in his appointment as director of the National Library just when he was no longer able to read the volumes he presided over. When we left the library for a walk on the Southside, the Buenos Aires of many of his poems, his one hand lightly in the crook of my arm, his stick ever present in the other, it was I who was seeing the city and reading the street signs, but it was Borges who provided the footnotes and the anecdotes. Sometimes, invoking a text, he paused as if leafing through a library in his head before finding the book and the page and haltingly bringing back the sentence or the line.

Around Borges in Buenos Aires I sensed a host of attendant spirits — waiters and taxi-drivers who knew his ways, friends ready to read to him or take his dictation, assistants in the library who watched over him — for now that his fame had spread to Europe and the United States he had become a national treasure. Passersby in the street murmured his name as a kind of salutation. I returned him to the library, to the guard who stood by the door. We said our goodbyes, and I moved out of the circle of his attention into the labyrinth of that inexhaustible city, of which he once wrote:

Hard to believe Buenos Aires had any beginning.
I feel it to be as eternal as air and water.

Although I then spent some days in Brazil, I realized that I had reached a kind of saturation, that I had enough to occupy my mind for a foreseeable time. So I made my way, by stages, back to Spain, where I unpacked my book hoard. In the late seventies, I was to do the reverse: pack and send books from the newly democratic Spain to friends in Chile and Argentina, both then in political darkness.

*

But at this time it was Spain that had become politically uncomfortable, and in late 1966 I returned to Britain, moving to London with my son, Jasper, to live for the next three years on a houseboat on the Thames at Chelsea Reach. Fastened to London only by our mooring, we felt ourselves to be something of an offshore island. We found many Latin American friends in London at that time, Mario Vargas Llosa and Guillermo Cabrera Infante among them. Sometimes the boat sounded like a Spanish American outpost moored to the Chelsea Embankment.

Earlier that year, I had met Emir Rodriguez Monegal, a longtime friend and chronicler of both Borges and Neruda. Emir — dark, sharp-faced, incisive, and with great charm — had just been appointed director of a new cultural review called *Mundo Nuevo*, which he edited from Paris. Emir came to England once a week to give a seminar at Cambridge, and regularly stopped off at the houseboat on the way. A prodigious and perceptive reader, he had realized that, at that particular moment in the countries of Spanish America, a number of extraordinary writers were surfacing, and that all at once a Latin American literature was coming into being, more than fulfilling the prediction that Carlos Barral had made in Barcelona. *Mundo Nuevo*, which, under

Monegal, ran to just twenty-five issues, is often credited with having launched the Boom. Emir published the work of Cabrera Infante, the brilliant Cuban writer who had just then sought political asylum in London, as well as the first fragment of García Márquez's *One Hundred Years of Solitude*. García Márquez was politically in sympathy with Neruda, and revered him as a poet, yet his book also shows everywhere the influence of Borges — in how it regards odd and magical happenings as natural events, and sees everywhere the collisions between private fictions and an unyielding reality.

The shadows of Neruda and Borges hung over the whole generation of writers that followed them — not so much as direct literary influences but as forerunners. Neruda held out his vision of a South American *continent*, sharing a turbulent history, a singular humanity, and a common plight. Borges swept away the previous restraints of realism by demonstrating that fiction creates a separate world, where a writer can make his own laws and create his own appropriate language. While Spanish America's younger writers mostly took their passion and politics from Neruda, it was Borges who reminded them of the magical nature of their craft. Emir once suggested to me that, just as Don Quixote and Sancho Panza, seen as sides of the same person, reflect the contradictions of the Spanish character, so the Spanish American psyche could be thought of as embracing the sensual immediacy of Neruda and the labyrinthine questionings of Borges.

Borges and Neruda gave extensive interviews to Rita

Guibert for a book she published in 1973 on Latin American writers. Of Borges's politics Neruda had this to say: 'If he thinks like a dinosaur, that has nothing to do with my thinking. He doesn't understand a thing about what's happening in the modern world, and he thinks that I don't either. Therefore, we are in agreement.' When Borges was questioned on his politics, he answered this way:

> My only commitment is to literature and my own sincerity. As for my political attitude, I've always made it perfectly clear: I've been anti-communist, anti-Hitler, anti-Peronist, and anti-nationalist . . . If a story or a poem of mine is successful, its success springs from a deeper source than my political views, which may be erroneous and are dictated by circumstances. In my case, my knowledge of what is called political reality is very incomplete. My life is really spent among books, many of them from a past age.

For Borges, an intellectual anarchist, politics took place in the street, not in his mind, yet he was not untouched by them. His family, professional and middle-class, traditionally voted conservative, and when the Second World War broke out they were emphatically pro-British. In 1946, Borges had made known in print his opposition to Juan Perón's dictatorship, which he saw as pro-Axis. He was dismissed from his post in a municipal library and appointed poultry inspector in a public market, a post he never filled but a humiliation

he never forgot. The military government that succeeded Perón, in 1955, made amends by appointing
Borges the director of the National Library, which was
tantamount to appointing him the national touchstone
he became.

*

From the sixties on, I translated a fair part of Borges's
poetry for various selections of his work; and I col-
laborated in an edition of Neruda's *Selected Poems*,
going on later to translate several single volumes of his.
Translating someone's work, poetry in particular, has
something about it akin to being possessed, haunted.
Translating a poem means not only reading it deeply
and deciphering it but clambering about backstage
among the props and the scaffolding. I found I could
no longer read a poem of Neruda's simply as words
on a page without hearing behind them that languid,
caressing voice. Most important to me in translating
these two writers was the sound of their voices in
my memory, for it very much helped in finding the
English appropriate to those voices. I found that if
I learned poems of Neruda's by heart I could replay
them at odd moments, on buses, at wakeful times in
the night, until, at a certain point, the translation
would somehow set. The voice was the clue: I felt
that all Neruda's poems were fundamentally vocative
— spoken poems, poems of direct address — and that
Neruda's voice was in a sense the instrument for which

he wrote. He once made a tape for me, reading pieces of different poems, in different tones and rhythms. I played it over so many times that I can hear it in my head at will. Two lines of his I used to repeat like a Zen koan, for they seemed to apply particularly to translating:

> in this net it's not just the strings that count
> but also the air that escapes through the meshes.

He often wrote of himself as having many selves, just as he had left behind him several very different poetic manners and voices. In talking to Rita Guibert, he explained his protean nature thus: 'If my poetry has any virtue it's that it's an organism, it's organic and emanates from my own body. When I was a child, my poetry was childish, it was youthful when I was young, despairing when I was suffering, aggressive when I had to take part in the social struggle, and there is still a mixture of all these different tendencies in the poetry I write now, which may perhaps be at the same time childish, aggressive, and despairing . . . I have always written from some inner necessity . . . I'm an anti-intellectual, I don't much care for analysis or for examining literary currents, and I'm not a writer who subsists on books, although books are necessary to my life.' His dutiful political poems are mainly forgettable, but occasionally the politics and the poetry come together, as in his meditation on food and hunger, 'The Great Tablecloth', which concludes:

Let us sit down soon to eat
with all those who haven't eaten,
let us spread great tablecloths,
put salt in the lakes of the world,
set up planetary bakeries,
tables with strawberries in snow,
and a plate like the moon itself
from which we will all eat.

For now I ask no more
than the justice of eating.

There is so much of Neruda in that single last couplet.

Then I would turn to the universe of Borges. Bringing his poetry into English was much more straightforward. Borges made constant use of certain English verse forms — rhymed quatrains and sonnets in particular — so that translating them required mainly a good ear and a certain prosodic agility in English. In the case of his sonnets, I was careful not to torture them into matching form in English — ingenuity at the expense of poetry. While Neruda's poems are wide-ranging, in their subject matter, their manner, their gesture, their tone, so that they must be taken singly, as separate events, Borges's poems are related to one another, not just in their formal manner and their heraldry of recurring symbols — chessboards, maps, knives, mirrors, coins, labyrinths, tigers, libraries — but in their sceptical, questioning undertone. They let you in on a secret, as observer, as eavesdropper. Translating Borges felt to me like learning a private language: the

exact cast of certain favourite words of his, like the
noun *olvido*, which he uses to mean either death or
sleep or forgetting, and of certain of his vertiginous
adjectives, has to be intuited every time. Borges is a
much less adventurous or original poet than Neruda:
for him, poetry is one of the several dimensions of
language he explored, and his poems are mainly parts
of a larger whole. He did, however, write a handful
of very memorable single poems, like his 'Matthew,
XXV:30', in which he imagines a voice confronting
him with the vocabulary of his own existence:

Stars, bread, libraries of East and West,
playing cards, chessboards, galleries, skylights, cellars,
a human body to walk with on the earth,
fingernails, growing at nighttime and in death,
shadows for forgetting, mirrors that endlessly multiply,
falls in music, gentlest of all time's shapes,
borders of Brazil, Uruguay, horses and mornings,
a bronze weight, a copy of Grettir Saga,
algebra and fire, the charge at Junín in your blood,
days more crowded than Balzac, scent of the honey-
                                        suckle,
love, and the imminence of love, and intolerable
                                        remembering,
dreams like buried treasure, generous luck,
and memory itself, where a glance can make
                                        men dizzy—

all this was given to you and, with it,
the ancient nourishment of heroes—

treachery, defeat, humiliation.
In vain have oceans been squandered on you, in vain
the sun, wonderfully seen through Whitman's eyes.
You have used up the years and they have used up
you,
and still, and still, you have not written the poem.

*

Pablo and Matilde turned up in London in 1967, and
when Pablo heard that I lived on a houseboat he
came straight to inspect it. He decided he must hold
his birthday fiesta there, an evening brimming with
Chileans, in the course of which a Ukrainian poet had
to be rescued from the Thames mud. I accompanied
Pablo to the street market in Petticoat Lane and to
a ship's chandler by the docks in a vain search for a
ship's figurehead. He was anxious to have me translate
the whole of *Estravagario*, a favourite book of his, and I
agreed with pleasure. In England, wrapped in a Chilean
poncho, Pablo looked unnaturally cold, but when we
gave a reading together in the Queen Elizabeth Hall I
listened to his voice spreading itself like a balm over the
English audience — a magical sound, even without the
string of sense. After the reading, he was courtesy itself,
while regularly casting a side glance in my direction,
dinner on his mind.

After being closeted for a spell with the still photographs of his poems, I found it a relief to spend time
with the moving original. I knew Neruda much better

now, by way of his poems. He was always ready to answer any questions I had about them, even to talk about them, fondly, as about lost friends, but he was not much interested in the mechanics of translation. Once, in Paris, while I was explaining some liberty I had taken, he stopped me and put his hand on my shoulder. 'Alastair, don't just translate my poems. I want you to improve them.'

In 1969, Neruda stood as Communist candidate for the Presidency of Chile, but after a brief campaign he dropped out and threw his support behind his friend Salvador Allende; and Allende, once elected, in 1970, appointed Neruda Chilean Ambassador to France. From then on, Pablo and I saw each other frequently, for he came to London every so often. We had an easy friendship: in his eyes, I, as translator, had joined his cast, and, although he became very much a public poet again, especially following his Nobel Prize in Literature, in 1971, he would shed his official self in the company of friends, as at a backstage party. In the vast Chilean Embassy in Paris, he ignored the voluminous public rooms and furnished a room in his own suite as a French café, with tables, wire chairs, and a zinc bar: it was there that diplomacy, politics, literature, and friendships were all enacted. I had been in Chile in his absence, and, having stayed in his house in Isla Negra, I brought him a full report on the state of the garden and on an extension being built while he was away. Then, late in 1972, he wrote me, saying that he was resigning and returning to Chile. His health had been failing, he explained, and he wanted to be attended to at home. The day of his homecoming was celebrated as a national holiday in Chile, but already, as he had hinted, ominous signs were in the air — not only of Neruda's deteriorating health but of a menacing opposition emerging in Chilean politics. Then, on September 11, 1973, the military coup savaged Chile, and twelve days later Neruda died of cancer in a clinic in Santiago. Now only the poems remained. The tape he had made me became, suddenly, like a precious relic, except that I had long since transferred it to my memory, where it never needed rewinding:

> It is time, love, to break off that sombre rose,
> shut up the stars and bury the ash in the earth;
> and, in the rising of the light, wake with those
> > awaking
> or go on in the dream, reaching the other shore of the
> > sea which has no other shore.

While Neruda was running for President in Chile, my son and I were living by the sea on the outskirts of St Andrews in Scotland, and there we received a letter from Borges announcing a forthcoming stop on his way to receive an honorary degree at Oxford. He arrived with Maria Kodama, a graceful, gentle Argentine woman of Japanese ancestry, who acted as his travelling companion, and whom he married, to the gratification of his friends, shortly before he died. He was much affected by being in Scotland, as though his reading had suddenly come to life. He took walks with my son beside the North Sea and pulled Border ballads from his memory. In those few unplanned days, he laid aside the obligation to be Borges, the public self to which his writings bound him, as he described it in his short fiction 'Borges and I':

> I live, I allow myself to live, so that Borges can unwind his writings, and these writings justify me ... Years ago, I tried to free myself from him and I went from writing down the myths of my district to devising games with time and infinity, but these games have become part of Borges by now, and I will have to think up something else ... I don't know which of us is writing this page.

By now, Borges was regularly accepting some of the many invitations that came his way — to lecture, to receive honorary degrees and cultural decorations, in Europe and the United States. Reverential audiences came to hear him, as if to confirm that he existed. Once, visiting him in Buenos Aires in 1978, I asked him about his sudden appetite for travel. 'When I am at home in Buenos Aires,' he told me, 'one day is much like another. But when I travel — and you must realize that for me, since I am blind, travelling means merely changing armchairs — friendly ghosts materialize one by one and talk to me about literature, and about my own writings, most generously. For a writer, that is great luxury. I feel blessed by it, I feel lucky.'

Borges had grown tired of lecturing, and when he visited New York, in the late seventies, he would sometimes telephone me and invite me to join him in giving a *charla* — a conversation onstage in which I would ask him questions inviting to his mind. He loved to talk of the hazards of translation: as he once wrote, 'Nothing is as consubstantial with literature and its modest mystery as the questions raised by a translation.' On these occasions, I would sometimes try to surprise him with a question, and as often as not he would surprise me back. I grew to know well a certain movement of his mind, in which he would first make a straightforward statement about a book or a writer and then, after a gravid pause, abruptly undermine it with an ironic afterthought, a subversive aside, mischievous, mocking, desolemnizing.

In 1985, in New York, Borges gave me a copy of a recent poem. It had no title, and after some deliberation he decided to call it 'The Web'. It began:

> Which of my cities
> am I doomed to die in?
> Geneva,
> where revelation reached me
> from Virgil and Tacitus?

My translation of the poem lay patiently in *The New Yorker* files until June of 1986, when it saw the light: I received a copy of the magazine while I was in Mexico City. Soon after, coming in from a walk, I switched on the television to find the Mexican poet Octavio Paz talking about Borges in the past tense. He had died earlier that day, in Geneva.

All that time, of occasional meetings interspersed with long periods of immersion in their texts, gave me a curious and complex connection to both of these men. Rereading them, I see always more clearly the interweaving of their writings and their lives — their poems as incarnations. I find nothing at all contradictory in accommodating them both. Borges used to say that when writers die they become books — a quite satisfactory incarnation in his view. With luck, however, I think they become voices. In many conversations with Borges, from the formal to the fanciful, I realized sharply that to him I existed only as a voice. That may have led to my deep conviction that voice is perhaps the most essential and lasting incarnation of any existence. More than that, it is in voices, far beyond photographs, that the dead continue to live. In the case of Neruda and Borges, their voices were for me the crucial, guiding element in my translating them. I think of their writings as encapsulations of their voices, and I hear them often in my head, always with awe, and with enduring affection.

POEMS III

TRANSLATIONS

In writing an original poem we are translating
the world, transmuting it.
  Everything we do is translation, and all
translations are in a way creations.

Octavio Paz

In this net it's not just the strings that count
but also the air that escapes through the meshes.

Pablo Neruda

What Gets Lost/Lo Que Se Pierde

I keep translating *traduzco continuamente*
entre palabras words *que no son las mias*
into other words which are mine *de palabras a mis*
palabras.

Y finalmente de quien es el texto?
Who do words belong to?
Del escritor o del traductor writer, translator
o de los idiomas or to language itself?
Traductores, somos fantasmas que viven
entre aquel mundo y el nuestro
translators are ghosts who live
in a limbo between two worlds
pero poco a poco me ocurre
que el problema no es cuestion
de lo que se pierde en traducion
the problem is not a question
of what gets lost in translation
sino but rather *lo que se pierde*
what gets lost
entre la ocurrencia — sea de amor o de agonia
between the happening of love or pain
y el hecho de que llega
a existir en palabras
and their coming into words.

Para nosotros todos, amantes, habladores
for lovers or users of words
el problema es este this is the difficulty—

lo que se pierde what gets lost
no es lo que se pierde en traducion sino
is not what gets lost in translation but more
what gets lost in language itself *lo que se pierde*
en el hecho en la lengua,
en la palabra misma.

SIX POEMS OF
JORGE LUIS BORGES

To Whoever is Reading Me

You are invulnerable. Have they not granted you,
those powers that preordain your destiny,
the certainty of dust? Is not your time
as irreversible as that same river
where Heraclitus, mirrored, saw the symbol
of fleeting life? A marble slab awaits you
which you will not read — on it, already written,
the date, the city, and the epitaph.
Other men, too, are only dreams of time,
not indestructible bronze or burnished gold;
the universe is, like you, a Proteus.
Dark, you will enter the darkness that expects you,
doomed to the limits of your travelled time.
Know that in some sense you are already dead.

The Other Tiger

And the craft createth a semblance.
—WM. MORRIS, *Sigurd the Volsung* (1876)

I think of a tiger. The twilight enhances
the vast complexities of the Library
and seems to set the bookshelves at a distance;

powerful, innocent, bloodstained, and new-made,
it will prowl through its jungle and its morning
and leave its footprint on the muddy edge
of a river with a name unknown to it
(in its world, there are no names, nor past, nor future,
only the sureness of the present moment)
and it will cross the wilderness of distance
and sniff out in the woven labyrinth
of smells the smell peculiar to morning
and the scent on the air of deer, delectable.
Behind the lattice of bamboo, I notice
its stripes, and I sense its skeleton
under the magnificence of the quivering skin.
In vain the convex oceans and the deserts
spread themselves across the earth between us;
from this one house in a far-off seaport
in South America, I dream you, follow you,
oh tiger on the fringes of the Ganges.

Evening spreads in my spirit and I keep thinking
that the tiger I am calling up in my poem
is a tiger made of symbols and of shadows,
a set of literary images,
scraps remembered from encyclopaedias,
and not the deadly tiger, the fateful jewel
that in the sun or the deceptive moonlight
follows its paths, in Bengal or Sumatra,
of love, of indolence, of dying.
Against the tiger of symbols I have set
the real one, the hot-blooded one

that savages a herd of buffalo,
and today, the third of August, 59,
a patient shadow moves across the plain,
but yet, the act of naming it, of guessing
what is its nature and its circumstance
creates a fiction, not a living creature,
not one of those that prowls on the earth.

Let us look for a third tiger. This one
will be a form in my dream like all the others,
a system, an arrangement of human language,
and not the flesh-and-bone tiger
that, out of reach of all mythologies,
paces the earth. I know all this; yet something
drives me to this ancient, perverse adventure,
foolish and vague, yet still I keep on looking
throughout the evening for the other tiger,
the other tiger, the one not in this poem.

Mirrors

I have been horrified before all mirrors,
not just before the impenetrable glass,
the end and the beginning of that space,
inhabited by nothing but reflections,

but faced with specular water, mirroring
the other blue within its bottomless sky,
incised at times by the illusory flight
of inverted birds, or troubled by a ripple,

or face to face with the unspeaking surface
of ghostly ebony whose very hardness
reflects, as if within a dream, the whiteness
of spectral marble or a spectral rose.

Now, after so many troubling years
of wandering underneath the wavering moon,
I ask myself what accident of fortune
handed to me this terror of all mirrors—

mirrors of metal and the shrouded mirror
of sheer mahogany which in the twilight
of its uncertain red softens the face
that watches and in turn is watched by it.

I look on them as infinite, elemental
fulfillers of a very ancient pact
to multiply the world, as in the act
of generation, sleepless and dangerous.

They extenuate this vain and dubious world
within the web of their own vertigo.
Sometimes at evening they are clouded over
by someone's breath, someone who is not dead.

The glass is watching us. And if a mirror
hangs somewhere on the four walls of my room,
I am not alone. There's an other, a reflection
which in the dawn enacts its own dumb show.

Everything happens, nothing is remembered
in those dimensioned cabinets of glass

in which, like rabbis in fantastic stories,
we read the lines of text from right to left.

Claudius, king for an evening, king in a dream,
did not know he was a dream until that day
on which an actor mimed his felony
with silent artifice, in a tableau.

Strange, that there are dreams, that there are mirrors.
Strange that the ordinary, worn-out ways
of every day encompass the imagined
and endless universe woven by reflections.

God, I've begun to think, implants a promise
in all that insubstantial architecture
that makes light out of the sheer surface
of glass, and lightens the dark dreams.

God has created nights well-populated
with dreams, crowded with mirror-images,
so that man may feel that he is nothing more
than vain reflection. That is what we fear.

Limits

Of all the streets that blur into the sunset,
there must be one (which, I am not sure)
that I by now have walked for the last time
without guessing it, the pawn of that Someone

who fixes in advance omnipotent laws,
sets up a secret and unwavering scale

for all the shadows, dreams, and forms
woven into the texture of this life.

If there is a limit to all things and a measure
and a last time and nothing more and forgetfulness,
who will tell us to whom in this house
we without knowing it have said farewell?

Through the dawning window night withdraws
and among the stacked books that throw
irregular shadows on the dim table,
there must be one which I will never read.

There is in the South more than one worn gate,
with its cement urns and planted cactus,
which is already forbidden to my entry,
inaccessible, as in a lithograph.

There is a door you have closed for ever
and some mirror is expecting you in vain;
to you the crossroads seem wide open,
yet watching you, four-faced, is a Janus.

There is among all your memories one
which has now been lost beyond recall.
You will not be seen going down to that fountain,
neither by white sun nor by yellow moon.

You will never recapture what the Persian
said in his language woven with birds and roses,
when, in the sunset, before the light disperses,
you wish to give words to unforgettable things.

And the steadily-flowing Rhone and the lake,
all that vast yesterday over which today I bend?
They will be as lost as Carthage,
scourged by the Romans with fire and salt.

At dawn I seem to hear the turbulent
murmur of crowds milling and fading away;
they are all I have been loved by, forgotten by;
space, time, and Borges now are leaving me.

Adrogué

Let no-one fear in the bewildering night
that I will lose my way among the borders
of dusky flowers that weave a cloth of symbols
appropriate to old nostalgic loves

or the sloth of afternoons — the hidden bird
forever whittling the same thin song,
the circular fountain and the summerhouse,
the indistinct statue and the hazy ruin.

Hollow in the hollow shade, the coach-house
marks (I know well) the insubstantial edges
of this particular world of dust and jasmine
so dear to Julio Herrera and Verlaine.

The shade is thick with the medicinal smell
of the eucalyptus trees, that ancient balm
which, beyond time and ambiguities
of language, brings back vanished country houses.

My step feels out and finds the anticipated
threshold. Its darkened limit is defined
by the roof, and in the chessboard patio
the water-tap drips intermittently.

On the far side of the doorways they are sleeping,
those who through the medium of dreams
watch over in the visionary shadows
all that vast yesterday and all dead things.

Each object in this venerable building
I know by heart — the flaking layers of mica
on that grey stone, reflected endlessly
in the recesses of a faded mirror,

and the lion head which holds an iron ring
in its mouth, and the multicoloured window glass,
revealing to a child the early vision
of one world coloured red, another green.

Far beyond accident and death itself
they endure, each one with its particular story,
but all this happens in the strangeness of
that fourth dimension which is memory.

In it and it alone do they exist,
the gardens and the patios. The past
retains them in that circular preserve
which at one time embraces dawn and dusk.

How could I have forgotten that precise
order of things both humble and beloved,

today as inaccessible as the roses
revealed to the first Adam in Paradise?

The ancient aura of an elegy
still haunts me when I think about that house—
I do not understand how time can pass,
I, who am time and blood and agony.

The Web

Which of my cities
am I doomed to die in?
Geneva,
where revelation reached me
from Virgil and Tacitus
(certainly not from Calvin)?
Montevideo,
where Luis Melián Lafinur,
blind and heavy with years,
died among the archives
of that impartial
history of Uruguay
he never wrote?
Nara,
where in a Japanese inn
I slept on the floor
and dreamed the terrible
image of the Buddha
I had touched without seeing

but saw in my dream?
Buenos Aires,
where I verge on being a foreigner?
Austin, Texas,
where my mother and I
in the autumn of '61
discovered America?
What language
am I doomed to die in?
The Spanish my ancestors used
to call for the charge, or to play *truco?*
The English of the Bible
my grandmother read from
at the edges of the desert?
What time will it happen?
In the dove-coloured twilight
when colour drains away,
or in the twilight of the crow
when night abstracts and simplifies
all visible things?
Or at an inconsequential moment—
two in the afternoon?
These questions are
digressions that stem not from fear
but from impatient hope.
They form part of the fateful web
of cause and effect
that no man can foresee,
nor any god.

SIX POEMS OF
PABLO NERUDA

Poetry

And it was at that age . . . poetry arrived
in search of me. I don't know, I don't know where
it came from, from winter or a river.
I don't know how or when,
no, they were not voices, they were not
words, not silence,
but from a street it called me,
from the branches of night,
abruptly from the others,
among raging fires
or returning alone,
there it was, without a face,
and it touched me.
I didn't know what to say, my mouth
had no way
with names,
my eyes were blind.
Something knocked in my soul,
fever or forgotten wings,
and I made my own way,
deciphering
that fire,
and I wrote the first, faint line,

faint, without substance, pure
nonsense,
pure wisdom
of someone who knows nothing,
and suddenly I saw
the heavens
unfastened
and open,
planets,
palpitating plantations,
the darkness perforated,
riddled
with arrows, fire, and flowers,
the overpowering night, the universe.

And I, tiny being,
drunk with the great starry
void,
likeness, image of
mystery,
felt myself a pure part
of the abyss.
I wheeled with the stars.
My heart broke loose with the wind.

Keeping Quiet

Now we will count to twelve
and we will all keep still.

For once on the face of the earth,
let's not speak in any language;
let's stop for one second,
and not move our arms so much.

It would be an exotic moment
without rush, without engines;
we would all be together
in a sudden strangeness.

Fishermen in the cold sea
would not harm whales
and the man gathering salt
would look at his hurt hands.

Those who prepare green wars,
wars with gas, wars with fire,
victories with no survivors,
would put on clean clothes
and walk about with their brothers
in the shade, doing nothing.

What I want should not be confused
with total inactivity.
Life is what it is about;
I want no truck with death.

If we were not so single-minded
about keeping our lives moving,
and for once could do nothing,
perhaps a huge silence
might interrupt this sadness

of never understanding ourselves
and of threatening ourselves with death.
Perhaps the earth can teach us
as when everything seems dead
and later proves to be alive.

Now I'll count up to twelve
and you keep quiet and I will go.

Dazzle of Day

Enough now of the wet eyes of winter.
Not another single tear.
Hour by hour now, green is beginning,
the essential season, leaf by leaf,
until, in spring's name, we are summoned
to take part in joy.

How wonderful, its eternal all-ness,
new air, the promise of flower,
the full moon leaving
its calling card in the foliage,
men and women trailing back from the beach
with a wet basket
of shifting silver.

Like love, like a medal,
I take in,
take in

south, north, violins,
dogs,
lemons, clay,
newly liberated air.
I take in machines smelling of mystery,
my storm-coloured shopping,
everything I need:
orange blossom, string,
grapes like topaz,
the smell of waves.
I gather up,
endlessly,
painlessly,
I breathe.
I dry my clothes in the wind,
and my open heart.
The sky falls
and falls.
From my glass,
I drink
pure joy.

Too Many Names

Mondays are meshed with Tuesdays
and the week with the whole year.
Time cannot be cut
with your exhausted scissors,

and all the names of the day
are washed out by the waters of night.

No-one can claim the name of Pedro,
nobody is Rosa or Maria,
all of us are dust or sand,
all of us are rain under rain.
They have spoken to me of Venezuelas,
of Chiles and Paraguays;
I have no idea what they are saying.
I know only the skin of the earth
and I know it has no name.

When I lived amongst the roots
they pleased me more than flowers did,
and when I spoke to a stone
it rang like a bell.

It is so long, the spring
which goes on all winter.
Time lost its shoes.
A year lasts four centuries.

When I sleep every night,
what am I called or not called?
And when I wake, who am I
if I was not I while I slept?

This means to say that scarcely
have we landed into life
than we are as if new-born;
let us not fill our mouths

with so many faltering names,
with so many sad formalities,
with so many pompous letters,
with so much of yours and mine,
with so much signing of papers.

I have a mind to confuse things,
unite them, make them new-born,
mix them up, undress them,
until all light in the world
has the oneness of the ocean,
a generous, vast wholeness,
a crackling, living fragrance.

The Great Tablecloth

When they were called to the table,
the tyrants came rushing
with their temporary ladies,
it was fine to watch the women pass
like wasps with big bosoms
followed by those pale
and unfortunate public tigers.

The peasant in the field ate
his poor quota of bread,
he was alone, it was late,
he was surrounded by wheat,
but he had no more bread;

he ate it with grim teeth,
looking at it with hard eyes.

In the blue hour of eating,
the infinite hour of the roast,
the poet abandons his lyre,
takes up his knife and fork,
puts his glass on the table,
and the fishermen attend
the little sea of the soup bowl.
Burning potatoes protest
among the tongues of oil.
The lamb is gold on its coals
and the onion undresses.
It is sad to eat in dinner clothes,
like eating in a coffin,
but eating in convents
is like eating underground.
Eating alone is a disappointment,
but not eating matters more,
is hollow and green, has thorns
like a chain of fish-hooks
trailing from the heart,
clawing at your insides.

Hunger feels like pincers,
like the bite of crabs,
it burns, burns and has no fire.
Hunger is a cold fire.
Let us sit down soon to eat
with all those who haven't eaten;

let us spread great tablecloths,
put salt in the lakes of the world,
set up planetary bakeries,
tables with strawberries in snow,
and a plate like the moon itself
from which we can all eat.

For now I ask no more
than the justice of eating.

Where Can Guillermina Be?

Where can Guillermina be?

When my sister invited her
and I went out to open the door,
the sun came in, the stars came in,
two tresses of wheat came in
and two inexhaustible eyes.

I was fourteen years old,
brooding, and proud of it,
slim, lithe and frowning,
funereal and formal.
I lived among the spiders,
dank from the forest,
the beetles knew me,
and the three-coloured bees.
I slept among partridges,
hidden under the mint.

Then Guillermina entered
with her blue lightning eyes
which swept across my hair
and pinned me like swords
against the wall of winter.
That happened in Temuco,
there in the South, on the frontier.

The years have passed slowly,
pacing like pachyderms,
barking like crazy foxes.
The soiled years have passed,
waxing, worn, funereal,
and I walked from cloud to cloud,
from land to land, from eye to eye,
while the rain on the frontier
fell in its same grey shape.

My heart has travelled
in the same faithful shoes,
and I have endured the thorns.
I had no rest where I was:
where I hit out, I was struck,
where they murdered me I fell;
and I revived, as fresh as ever,
and then and then and then and then—
it all takes so long to tell.

I have nothing to add.

I came to live in this world.

Where can Guillermina be?

Translator to Poet

For Pablo Neruda, 1904–73

There are only the words left now. They lie like
                                            tombstones
or the stone Andes where the green scrub ends.
I do not have the heart to chip away
at your long lists of joy, which alternate
their iron and velvet, all the vegetation
and whalebone of your chosen stormy coast.
So much was written hope, with every line
extending life by saying, every meeting
ending in expectation of the next.
It was your slow intoning voice which counted,
bringing a living Chile into being
where poetry was bread, where books were banquets.
Now they are silent, stony on the shelf.
I cannot read them for the thunderous silence,
the grief of Chile's dying and your own,
death being the one definitive translation.

Other People's Houses

Having been, for many years, an itinerant, I am no stranger to other people's houses. I am aware of a certain disreputable cast to this admission; I can almost feel my wizened little ancestors shaking their heads and wringing their hands, for in Scotland, people tend to go from the stark stone house where they first see the light to another such fortress, where they sink roots and prepare dutifully for death, their possessions encrusted around them like barnacles. Anyone who did not seem to be following the stone script was looked on as somewhat raffish, rather like the tinkers and travelling people who sometimes passed through the village where I grew up. I would watch them leave, on foot, over the horizon, pulling their worldly belongings behind them in a handcart; and one of my earliest fantasies was to run away with them, for I felt oppressed by permanence and rootedness, and my childhood eyes strayed always to the same horizon, which promised other ways of being, a life less stony and predictable.

My errant nature was confirmed by a long time I spent at sea during the Second World War, on a series of small, cramped ships, wandering all over the Indian Ocean. Then I learned that the greatest advantage was to have as little as possible, for anything extra usually got lost or stolen, and we frequently had to shoulder our worldly goods, from ship to ship. The habit stuck — today I have next to no possessions, and I have closed the door on more houses and apartments than I can remember, leaving behind what I did not immediately need. If I had a family crest, it should read *omnia mea mecum porto* (all that is mine I carry with me); but it would get left behind.

Innocent in themselves, houses can be given quite different auras, depending on the dispositions of their occupants — they can be seen as monuments to permanence, or as temporary shelters. In Scotland, you find abundant examples of the first on the fringes of small towns, standing in well-groomed gardens, their brasses gleaming, their blinds half-drawn like lowered eyelids, domestic museums served by near-invisible slaves. When I first came to the United States, I felt it to be immediately liberating, in its fluidity, its readiness to change. Few people lived in the place they were born, moving held no terrors, and renting was the norm. Yet people inhabited their temporary shelters as though they might live there forever; and paradoxically, I felt at home. When I began to spend a part of each year in Spain, my other adopted country, I rented a series of sturdy peasant houses devoid of decoration, with whitewashed walls and tile floors, and no furnishings beyond the essentials of beds, tables, cross, and chairs. It was a time when a number of unanchored people came to rest in Spain — painters for the light, writers for the silence — setting up working outposts in the sun, whose constant presence does simplify existence. Within these anonymous white walls, one re-created one's own world — essential books and pictures, whatever other transforming elements lay to hand.

In Spain, I grew very aware of houses as presences — perhaps the residual aura of those who had lived lifetimes in them, perhaps a peculiarity of the space they enclosed. I recall visiting a house in Majorca in the company of Robert Graves, and hearing him, after only a few minutes in the house, making peremptory excuses to leave. 'Didn't you feel the bad luck in that house?' he said to me once we were out of earshot. With time, I came to feel what he meant, not in terms of good or bad luck, but of feeling welcome or unwelcome in the houses themselves, apart from the inhabitants.

Of all writers, Vladimir Nabokov read the interiors of other people's houses much as psychics read palms or tarot cards: with a wicked accuracy, he would decipher absent owners from the contents of rooms, from shelves, pictures, and paraphernalia. When he lectured at Cornell University, it was his practice, instead of having a house of his own, to rent the houses of others absent on sabbatical; and behind him already was a wandering life of exile in England, Germany, and France, in rented premises. Summers he spent in pursuit of butterflies, in motels across the United States; and when, with recognition, he came to rest, it was in a hotel apartment in Montreux, Switzerland.

These various houses and interiors inhabit his books as vividly as living characters — he is always making precise connections between people and the places they choose to live in, between objects and their owners. His *Look at the Harlequins!* is a positive hymn to other people's houses.

I know just what he means. The act of inhabiting and humanizing a house, of changing it from impersonal space to private landscape, is an extremely complex one, a series of careful and cumulative choices; and, in living in other people's houses, one lives among their decisions, some inspired, others hardly thought through. I make for the bookshelves with a crow of expectation, for the books, however miscellaneous or specialized they may be, always yield up at least a handful I have never read, or even heard of, and travelling has deprived me of the possibility of keeping a library, beyond a shelf of essential or immediate reading. Kitchens are a less calculable adventure. Some of them are like shrines, where cooking has been raised to a level of high art, and invite culinary adventure; others, incomprehensibly, are as bare as hospital labs in plague-prone countries, their refrigerators bearing no more than a few viruses flourishing in jars, two or three bottles of what can only be assumed to be an antidote.

At one point in our lives, my son and I lived in London, on a houseboat we actually owned, though temporarily, moored at Cheyne Walk, in Chelsea. We had three special friends, families that lived in other parts of London; and we came to an arrangement with them to exchange houses from time to time, for appropriate weekends. We had a loose agreement — we left behind clean sheets and towels, a 'reasonable amount' of food and drink, and, for the curious, some correspondence that could be read. We all relished these unlikely vacations, since we left one another elaborately written guidebooks, and we could take in another part of London — markets, greengrocers, pubs, restaurants. I often wonder why people never think of doing that oftener, except at the wrong times.

In our travels, my son and I occupied rented houses and apartments from Barcelona to Buenos Aires. He can remember every one of them in detail, down to its sounds — the creak and shudder of the houseboat as it rose off the Thames mud on the incoming tide, a house in Chile with a centre patio cooled by the cooing of doves, a cottage in Scotland in a wood of its own, guarded by a cranky tribe of crows, and the small mountain house in Spain that was our headquarters. Moving was like putting on different lives, different clothes, and we changed easily, falling in with the ways of each country, eating late in Spain, wearing raincoats in Scotland, carrying little from one place to another except the few objects that had become talismans, observing the different domestic rites — of garden and kitchen, mail and garbage.

Since the fifties, I have lived off and on in many different parts of New York, but very intermittently, since I came and went from Spain and from Scotland, never settling decisively in any one of the three. This fall, I returned from a summer spent in Scotland with no apartment — I had given one up before I left, and was expecting another in the spring; but a friend of mine, a dancer, was to be away for a month, and offered me her place in the East Village. I moved in, and took stock.

The apartment itself immediately felt lucky to me, the kind of apartment you want to stay *in* in, with high windows looking out over St Mark's churchyard, and light filtered in through leaves to a white, high-ceilinged room, with about a third of the books new to me, and a long Indian file of records. I fell in happily with the place, explored the neighbourhood, and found its Meccas — a Ukrainian butcher shop, pawnshops fat with the appliances of yesteryear, small Indian restaurants that looked as though they might fold themselves up after dinner and silently steal away. I made half-hearted attempts to find a more lasting sublet — buying the *Village Voice* early on Wednesdays, marking up the *Times* real-estate section on Sunday and then losing it — but that place made me immune to urgency, although St Mark's chimed the hours in my ear.

One evening, I was having dinner with a friend of mine, a camerawoman, who lives in a loft in SoHo. She moves fast and often, and always seems to be attached to the ends of five or six active wires, so when we have dinner, we have a lot of ground to cover. Over dessert, she suddenly sat up straight. 'By the way, I have to shoot in Arizona most of October. Do you know anyone who would stay in my loft and look after my cats?' We made a deal there and then; and, in a flash, I could see the shape of fall changing. Looking out reflectively on the churchyard the following morning, I realized that I was ideally equipped to be an itinerant. I have an office at the *New Yorker* magazine, where I keep books and papers, get my mail, and do my writing, when the time is upon me. What furniture remained to me now graced my son's apartment, and I was portable, to the tune of two small bags. I was in touch with other itinerants, some of whom would likely be going somewhere; and I was myself leaving for South America after Christmas, until the spring. So I dropped the *Voice*, and went back to reading Michel Tournier's *Friday and Robinson: Life on Esperanza Island*, my latest bookshelf discovery.

I had never lived in SoHo, and my translation there in October opened it up to me. I had to have a small course of initiation, in the hand elevator, in the fistful of keys, in the cats, and then I saw my friend off in a welter of camera gear — a less portable profession, hers, compared to writing. But then, I have always given thanks that I did not play the harp. The cats. Alvin, the boss-cat was called, a massive, broad-shouldered animal who looked as if he might lift weights in secret. Sadie, his sidekick, was smaller and dumber, but she simpered and purred, which Alvin never did.

Every morning, I fed them first thing, grinding up liver, cleaning their dishes; and when I came back in the evening, they would collar me and drive me toward their empty bowls. The first Saturday, Alvin got through plastic, paper, and close to a pound of sole when I wasn't looking, about an hour after his ample breakfast. But cats are unpunishable by nature, and we came to terms, which meant that I fed them just enough to keep them from breaking into those nerve-rending cries of simulated starvation. Cats in SoHo have the best life going, I concluded, in a loft that must have seemed like an Olympic complex to them, with me to do the shopping. Sometimes I wished they would go out jogging. But I found I could take a brisk walk without leaving the loft, and there was cable television, which kept me up the first couple of nights. Out in the street I learned to stroll all over again, and I connected up SoHo with the rest of Manhattan. I even took to working there, learning how Alvin and Sadie spent their day.

By then, I had come to count on what John Osborne once called 'the blessed alchemy of word of mouth', that most human of networks, and it put me in touch with a poet-friend, who was to be away giving readings for a spell in November. Could I stay and look after their plants? Unlike Alvin and Sadie, the plants fed slowly, in a slow seep; and I grew attached to one small fern that required drowning every day, and that rewarded me with new green. Their apartment was in the West Village, the part of New York I have lived in most. The stores were familiar, the kitchen a pleasure to cook in, the books unsurpassable, almost all of them good to read or reread. You can count on poets. Eerily enough, I had stayed in the same apartment once before, on a quick visit from Spain in the sixties, when other friends occupied it. Now it was dressed altogether differently; but every so often, I caught a whiff of its old self and experienced a time warp, with the kind of involuntary start that often becomes a poem in the end.

As my days there were beginning to be countable, another friend called me, a woman who writes often on Latin America. She was going to Honduras quite soon, and she had two questions: Did I know anyone in Tegucigalpa? Did I know anyone who wanted to rent her apartment for December, while she was gone? Yes to both questions; and, a couple of weeks later, I gave her two addresses in exchange for her keys.

There was, however, a spell in November, between cats, plants, and travels, and also between apartments, when I was saved from the streets by being able to find a room on the Upper East Side. I was finishing a piece on writing at the time, working a long day; but even so I never became a familiar of the Upper East Side, never have. It is hardly itinerants' territory. People don't stroll much there — they seem more purposive, and you have to know where the stores are. You don't stumble on them. It was getting difficult, too, with the subways — I had to think, really *think*, where I was living, Uptown or Downtown, not to go hurtling on the subway in a wrong though familiar direction.

My last resting place lay on the Upper West Side, also a new territory to me, since I have always thought of Forty-fifth Street as the Northern Frontier. It was, however, a revelation. There were oases of movie theaters, comforting even though I never went inside, plenty of odd stores to stumble on, and the neighbourhood, to my delight, was Spanish-speaking, even rich in Dominicans, the pleasantest people in Christendom. Moreover, a number of people I had always thought of as out of range turned out to live around the corner. I had had a hasty airport call from my Honduras-bound landlady that morning. 'Just pile the papers so you can walk around,' she told me tersely. Indeed, her apartment looked as though the negotiations over the Panama Canal had just been hastily concluded in it.

I cleared a camping space first, and then I put the place in order. I have a stern morality about occupying other people's houses: I feel they have to be left in better shape than I find them, and this may mean fixing faucets or supplying anything missing, from light bulbs to balloons. What her apartment needed was restoring to its original order, now only skeletally visible. Anyone who tries to keep up with Central America these days acquires a weekly layer of new information, and her layers went back a few months. When I had the papers rounded up and corralled, the books and records in their shelves and sleeves, the cups and glasses steeping, the place began to emerge and welcome me, and I found, under the sofa, an Anne Tyler novel I had not read. One thing did puzzle me: as I cleaned, I came everywhere on scatters of pennies, on the floor, on chairs, on desk and table, by the bed. I could not account for their ubiquity, but I gathered them in a jar, about enough to buy a good dinner. Christmas was coming to the Upper West Side, with great good cheer; but so was the cold weather, so I went one morning, and booked my air ticket.

Before I left the city, I retraced my wanderings of the fall, going home again and again. If you have lived in somebody's house, after all, you have acquired a lot in common with them, a lot to talk about, from the eccentricities of their pipes to the behaviour of their furniture. The tree house by St Mark's looked properly seasonal, with a fire burning. I find I can still occupy it in my head, with pleasure. I went by the West Village, sat talking for hours in the kitchen, and then walked down to SoHo, where I called on Alvin and Sadie, who looked keenly to see if I had brought fish before withdrawing to rest up. I dropped off a winter coat with my son, and made for the airport and the warm weather with my two bags, leaving behind not one city but several, I felt, shedding a cluster of distinct lives. I just had time to call my friend, newly back from Tegucigalpa. Her time had been good, yes, she had talked at length with my friends, the apartment was great, thanks for fixing the closet door, I had turned up things she thought she'd lost, she felt maybe she had caught a bug in Honduras. I asked her about the pennies. 'Oh, yes, thanks for picking them up,' she laughed. 'It's just that I throw the *I Ching* a lot. Have a good trip.'

In Memoriam, Amada

Judas Roquín told me this story, on the veranda of his
mildewed house in Cahuita. Years have passed and I
may have altered some details. I cannot be sure.

In 1933, the young Brazilian poet Baltasar Melo published a book of poems, *Brasil Encarnado*, which stirred
up such an outrage that Melo, forewarned by powerful
friends, chose to flee the country. The poems were
extravagant, unbridled even, in their manner, and applied
a running sexual metaphor to Brazilian life; but it was one
section, 'Perversions', in which Melo characterized three
prominent public figures as sexual grotesques, that made
his exile inevitable. Friends hid him until he could board
a freighter from Recife, under cover of darkness and an
assumed name, bound for Panama. With the ample
royalties from his book, he was able to buy an *estancia*
on the Caribbean coast of Costa Rica, not far from where
Roquín lived. The two of them met inevitably, though
they did not exactly become friends.

Already vain and arrogant by nature, Melo became
insufferable with success and the additional aura of
notorious exile. He used his fame mainly to entice women
with literary pretensions, some of them the wives of high
officials. In Brazil, however, he remained something of a
luminary to the young, and his flight added a certain
allure to his reputation, to such a point that two young

Bahian poets who worked as reporters on the newspaper *Folha da Tarde* took a leave of absence to interview him in his chosen exile. They travelled to Costa Rica mostly by bus, taking over a month to reach San José, the capital. Melo's retreat was a further day's journey, and they had to cover the last eleven kilometres on foot. Arriving at evening, they announced themselves to the housekeeper. Melo, already half-drunk, was upstairs, entertaining the daughter of a campesino, who countenanced the liaison for the sake of his fields. Melo, unfortunately, chose to be outraged, and shouted, in a voice loud enough for the waiting poets to hear, 'Tell those compatriots of mine that Brazil kept my poems and rejected me. Poetic justice demands that they return home and wait there for my next book.' For the two frustrated pilgrims, the journey back to Bahia was nothing short of nightmare.

*

The following autumn, a letter arrived in Cahuita for Baltasar Melo from a young Bahian girl, Amada da Bonavista, confessing shyly that her reading of *Brasil Encarnado* had altered her resolve to enter a convent, and asking for the poet's guidance. Flattered, titillated, he answered with a letter full of suggestive warmth. In response to a further letter from her, he made so bold as to ask for her likeness, and received in return the photograph of an irresistible beauty. Over the course of a whole year, their correspondence grew increasingly more erotic until, on impulse, Melo had his agent send her a steamship ticket from Bahia to Panama, where he proposed to meet her. Time passed, trying his patience; and then a letter arrived, addressed in an unfamiliar hand, from an aunt of Amada's. She had contracted meningitis and was in a critical condition. Not long after, the campesino's daughter brought another envelope with a Bahia postmark. It contained the steamship ticket, and a newspaper clipping announcing Amada's death.

We do not know if the two poets relished their intricate revenge, for they remain nameless, forgotten. But although it would be hard nowadays to track down an available copy of *Brasil Encarnado*, Baltasar Melo's name crops up in most standard anthologies of modern Brazilian poetry, represented always by the single celebrated poem, 'In Memoriam, Amada', which Brazilian schoolchildren still learn by heart. I translate, inadequately of course, the first few lines:

> Body forever in bloom,
> you are the only one
> who never did decay
> go grey, wrinkle, and die
> as all warm others do.
> My life, as it wears away
> owes all its light to you . . .

When Judas had finished, I of course asked him the inevitable question: Did Baltasar Melo ever find out? Did someone tell him? Roquín got up suddenly from the hammock he was sprawled in, and looked out to the white edge of surf, just visible under the rising moon. 'Ask me another time,' he said. 'I haven't decided yet.'